CRITICAL THINKING FOR TEENS

CRITICAL THINKING FOR TEENS

5 Secrets to Manage Peer Pressure, Make Smart Choices, Use Social Media Safely & Problem-Solve like a Pro to Build a Strong Foundation for Life

Andrea Campbell

Copyright © 2025 by Andrea Campbell 2025 - All rights reserved.

The content contained in this book may not be reproduced, duplicated, or transmitted without direct written permission from the author or publisher, except as permitted by U.S. copyright law.

Under no circumstances will any blame or legal responsibility be held against the publisher or author for any damages, reparation, or monetary loss due to the information contained within this book, either directly or indirectly. You are responsible for your own choices, actions, and results.

Legal Notice: This book is copyright-protected and is only for personal use. You cannot amend, distribute, sell, use, quote, or paraphrase any part of this book's content without the author's or publisher's consent.

Disclaimer Notice: Please note that the information contained in this text is for educational and entertainment purposes only. All effort has been executed to present accurate, up-to-date, and reliable, complete information. No warranties of any kind are declared or implied. Readers acknowledge that the author is not engaging in rendering legal, financial, medical, or professional advice. The content within this book has been derived from various sources.

ISBN: 978-1-914997-50-1 (sc)   978-1-914997-51-8 (hc)

Acknowledgements

Thanks to my family for their patience, love, and support. Your encouragement was the driving force that kept me going, and your belief in me made all the difference in bringing this book to fruition. I am endlessly grateful for your presence in my life.

A heartfelt thank you to Rajesh Kumar for your expertise and invaluable assistance in securing the photos featured in this book. Your dedication and knowledge helped bring my vision to life, and I truly appreciate your generosity and skill.

My appreciation and thanks Anna Smith, whose keen eye for detail and thoughtful insights helped shape this book into its best version. Your expertise, patience, and commitment to clarity and precision have been invaluable.

Dedication

I dedicate this book to my teenage daughter, Shasha, who has been a constant source of inspiration.

Her curiosity, resilience, and unique perspective have shaped the heart of this book, making it not just a guide for teens but also a reflection of the value and contribution of young people with congenital and neurodiverse conditions to society.

Contents

Introduction	IX
1. Lay of the Land: Setting out in Critical Thinking	3
2. Putting down Roots: Building a Strong Foundation for Thought	11
3. A Bird's Eye View: Seeing the Bigger Picture	25
4. Barking Up the Wrong Tree: Recognizing Reliable Sources	37
5. Seeing the Wood for the Trees: Gaining Perspective	51
6. Finding the Right Track: Analyzing Information Effectively	61
7. The Grass is Always Greener: Appreciating Different Viewpoints	75
8. Hidden Thorns: Spotting Common Thinking Traps	87
9. An Olive Branch: Approaching Conflicts Wisely	97

10. The Ripple Effect: Understanding Cause and Effect	111
11. Park Benches: The Power of Pause and Reflection	123
12. A Ray of Sunshine: Finding Optimism and Insight	133
13. The Community Garden: The Power of Collaborative Thinking	147
14. Beyond the Beaten Path: Applying Critical Thinking to Real Life	157
Conclusion	175
About the Author	178
Resources	179

Introduction

Life holds several lessons, and sometimes, the best classroom isn't inside four walls—it's out in the open, where nature provides the perfect setting for reflection and growth. This book is based on the frequent walks my teenage daughter Shasha and I take through our local nature reserve.

The reserve is home to a beautiful lake, an island where birds gather, and winding trails that lead to discoveries. The park is a place of discovery, where every visit brings new experiences, from watching the ripples to observing how birds behave in the changing seasons. These walks have become more than just a routine for us; they are opportunities to explore ideas, reflect on choices, and uncover valuable life lessons.

We make decisions, manage challenges, and encounter unexpected turns. How we think about and respond to these moments can shape our lives. Critical thinking isn't just about solving complex problems—it's about learning to interact with the world, ask the right questions, and make thoughtful choices. But where do we start?

For me, the answer can be found in nature. Shasha has special educational needs, and she finds these walks therapeutic. The sights, sounds, and experiences of the nature reserve give her a profound sense of calm and curiosity. The fresh air, the open space, and the simple act of moving through the natural world bring her joy and a deep sense of peace. As we stroll, we talk about what we notice in our surroundings. Over time, I realized that these walks were more than just an escape from the busyness of daily life. They were a way to teach valuable life lessons, and those moments inspired the information shared in this book.

We take you on a stroll in the park, using nature metaphors to explore key aspects of critical thinking. In the same way that the landscape changes from shaded treks to open fields and stony paths, our ability to think critically adapts to different life situations. Throughout these chapters, you will find information that will help you develop key problem-solving, decision-making, and critical-thinking skills. You'll gain essential life skills, such as resisting peer pressure and staying safe online. These abilities will help you manage challenges as a teenager and serve you well in adulthood and throughout your life. Through stories, reflections, and exercises, you'll learn to step back and see the bigger picture, recognize patterns, ask the right questions, and confidently make decisions.

Critical thinking is your key to unlocking new possibilities, whether figuring out the best path to take in life, learning to analyze information, or understanding different perspectives. Like the trails in the park, life offers many other routes, and your choices will shape your experience. The development of critical thinking can be challenging as well as exciting. There will be times when you might feel lost or unsure, and that's completely normal. The key is to keep exploring, stay curious, and trust that each step forward makes you stronger and wiser. In the coming chapters, you'll learn specific techniques, practice with real-life scenarios, and develop skills that will help you in your teen years and adult life. You will note that the book is divided into five parts; these represent the five secrets.

The pictures in the book were taken by me during my visits to the nature reserve near to my home in London, UK. The inspirational quotes are my intellectual property which you are welcome to use; please remember to attribute them to me.

By the end of this book, you'll be a better thinker and a more confident, creative, and adaptable person. You'll feel empowered to manage life's twists and turns with clarity, curiosity, and confidence. Let's go forward together and explore the lessons nature has to offer. There's so much to see, discover, and experience.

Part I

Lay a Foundation for Critical Thinking

It's better to walk away
limping than to stand
firm in the wrong place.

—*Andrea Campbell*

Chapter One

Lay of the Land: Setting out in Critical Thinking

Every journey begins in the mind, and then there is a first step. Critical thinking is no different. But before we set out, it's crucial to take stock of where we are, where we want to go, and what tools we'll need. We started our walk around our local park and stood at the edge of the lake to survey the landscape. It is a vast area containing a lake where swans, ducks, geese, pigeons, and other birds assemble. There is an outdoor gym, a playground, a tennis court, a cricket pitch, and football fields. The paths twist and turn through trees, hills, and grassland. It is beautiful indeed.

Picture yourself standing at the entrance of a vast nature reserve you've never explored. Each route offers different experiences and discoveries. This is precisely where you are right now with critical thinking—at the start of an exhilarating adventure that will change how you see and interact with the world.

What Is Critical Thinking?

Critical thinking isn't just about solving complex puzzles or debating intellectual ideas. It's a practical skill you use daily—when deciding which route to take to school, whether to trust something you read online or how to approach a disagreement with a friend. Critical thinking is your mental toolkit for understanding the world and making wise choices. It's not a distant concept but a tool that empowers you to solve problems, spot nonsense, and figure out what's happening around you.

Think about your favorite video game character leveling up. Each new level brings new abilities and tools to handle more significant challenges. Critical thinking is your real-life level-up system, and it's not a one-time thing. The more you practice, the better you get at spotting patterns and connections others miss and finding creative solutions to tricky problems. It will also help you make informed decisions and understand why people (including you) think and act as they do. Remember, it's not just a one-off event but a continuous action that requires commitment and persistence.

This chapter will help you lay the groundwork for becoming a better thinker, equipping you with the curiosity and confidence to navigate life's complexities.

What Does Critical Thinking Look Like?

Imagine standing at the edge of the lake in the nature reserve. The water looks calm on the surface, but if you look closely, you'll notice ripples from a bird landing, fish darting beneath the water, or the way sunlight dances on the waves. Critical thinking is about seeing those details and understanding how they connect.

At its core, critical thinking involves:

- *Observation*: Paying attention to what's happening around you.

- *Questioning*: Asking thoughtful questions to deepen your understanding.

- *Analyzing*: Breaking down information to uncover patterns and meanings.

- *Evaluating*: Assessing the quality of information, ideas, or solutions.

- *Communicating*: Expressing your thoughts clearly and listening to others.

Critical thinking isn't about being overly critical or doubting everything. Instead, it's about approaching situations with curiosity and an open mind while being thoughtful and discerning. Critical thinking motivates us to question, challenge, and think for ourselves, especially when the obvious answer isn't enough. It gives us the confidence and control to venture into uncharted territories.

Why Critical Thinking Matters

Think of life as that sprawling nature reserve with paths leading to different destinations. Some paths are straightforward, while others twist and turn, leading to unexpected challenges. Getting lost or wandering aimlessly is easy without a clear sense of direction. Critical thinking acts as your map and compass, guiding you toward thoughtful decisions and meaningful actions.

In a world overflowing with information, it can be hard to separate fact from fiction and wisdom from noise. Daily, we're bombarded with headlines, advertisements, social media posts, and opinions from people around us. Critical thinking helps you pause, question, and evaluate. It empowers you to discern what's valuable and filter out what isn't.

Beyond decision-making, critical thinking enhances creativity, fosters better relationships, and equips you to solve problems effectively. It allows you to see the bigger picture, understand other perspectives, and adapt to new situations—skills that will serve you in school, work, and life.

Forest area of the reserve

Starting Out: Assessing the Terrain

Before becoming a skilled critical thinker, you must understand where you are. Take a moment to reflect on these questions:

- Do you usually accept information at face value or question it?

- When faced with a problem, how do you approach finding a solution?

- How comfortable are you with changing your mind if new evidence emerges?

These questions aren't meant to judge but to give you a sense of your starting point. Just as a trek around the reserve begins with a quick landscape survey, understanding your current habits and tendencies will help you navigate the steps ahead.

You might think, "Okay, but why does this matter to me now?" Here's the deal: you're at a point in your life where you're starting to make more of your own decisions. Big decisions that can shape your future.

If you want to:

- Figure out what you want to do with your life
- Stop falling for fake news and social media manipulation
- Handle conflicts with friends and family better
- Make choices you'll be proud of later
- Stand out in school and future job applications

Critical thinking is your secret weapon for all of these.

Clearing the Path & Overcoming Common Obstacles

Fallen branches or muddy patches can block the paths in the reserve; in the same way, the road to becoming a better thinker has its challenges. Here are a few common obstacles and how to overcome them:

1. *Bias*: Everyone has biases—preferences or assumptions that influence our thinking. The key is recognizing them and questioning how they might affect your judgment.

2. *Overconfidence*: Believing you're right without questioning your assumptions is easy. Stay humble and be open to new information.

3. *Distractions*: In today's fast-paced world, distractions are everywhere. Make time to think deeply without interruptions.

4. *Fear of Being Wrong*: Making mistakes is part of learning. Instead of fearing failure, view it as an opportunity to grow.

Mapping Out Your Path

As we begin our study together, it's helpful to think of critical thinking as a series of stepping stones. Each chapter in this book builds on the last, helping you develop skills to serve you throughout life. Here's a preview of what lies ahead:

- *Foundation*: Understanding the basics of critical thinking and building strong habits.

- *Exploration*: Learning to observe, question, and analyze the world around you.

- *Decision-Making*: Mastering the art of making thoughtful choices.

- *Growth*: Learning key concepts of critical thinking

- *Application*: Applying critical thinking to challenges, relationships, and goals.

Shasha and I always take a moment at the start of our walks to enjoy the view and set an intention for the day. As you proceed in this book, take a moment to reflect on what you hope to gain. Maybe you want to make better decisions, solve problems more creatively, or understand yourself and others better.

Whatever your goal, know you're already taking an important step by reading this book. The path ahead is full of discovery, growth, and insight. Together, we'll explore the concepts and unlock the incredible power of your mind.

Let's head into Chapter 2, where we'll put down some firm roots for your critical thinking skills.

Key Takeaways from Chapter 1

1. **Critical thinking is a practical, everyday skill** - not just for academic debates but for daily decisions like choosing routes, evaluating online information, and navigating friendships.

2. **It's your mental toolkit for understanding the world** - helping you solve problems, spot nonsense, and make sense of what's happening around you.

3. **Critical thinking involves five core skills**: observation, questioning, analyzing, evaluating, and communicating.

4. **Like leveling up in a video game**, critical thinking skills improve with practice and unlock your ability to spot patterns others miss.

5. **In a world flooded with information**, critical thinking helps you separate fact from fiction and wisdom from noise.

6. **Common obstacles to critical thinking** include bias, overconfidence, distractions, and fear of being wrong - but all can be overcome with awareness.

7. **Critical thinking is your secret weapon** for navigating big life decisions, avoiding manipulation, handling conflicts better, and making choices you'll be proud of later.

Quick Reflection Questions:

1. What's one situation in your life where you could use better critical thinking?

2. What's your biggest challenge in developing your critical thinking skills?

Chapter Two

Putting down Roots: Building a Strong Foundation for Thought

In the serene nature reserve, trees stand tall and steady, their roots anchoring them to the earth. These roots, unseen but vital, draw nutrients from the soil and provide stability against the elements. Just as a tree's strength lies in its roots, your ability to think critically depends on the strength of your mental foundation.

Similarly, your ability to think critically depends on the strength of your mental foundation. Shasha and I observed trees of different types and sizes co-existing around the park. Some of these trees provided shade, while others were in areas where it was difficult to access. Some roots could be seen above the earth yards away from the foot of the trees. They kept the trees sturdy and safe from strong winds and other forces of nature.

This chapter explores how to establish roots to support your critical thinking process. In the same way that a tree's growth depends on the quality of its soil, the depth of its roots, and the conditions around it, your growth as a thinker relies on cultivating curiosity, embracing a growth mindset, and grounding yourself in solid principles of reasoning.

Trees plagued by parasites but standing strong and resilient

What Does It Mean to Put Down Roots?

Putting down roots is about more than just acquiring knowledge. It's about developing habits, attitudes, and practices that anchor your thinking. When your thoughts are rooted in curiosity, clarity, and logic, you'll find it easier to stay steady in the face of challenges and uncertainty.

Imagine a tree with shallow roots. It may appear fine on the surface, but a strong gust of wind could uproot it entirely. Similarly, without a strong foundation, your thinking can be swayed by emotions, biases, or misinformation. Putting down roots ensures your thoughts remain balanced, steady, and well-supported.

Root Habits of Critical Thinkers

Have you ever noticed how the oldest, sturdiest trees in a park have great big roots? These roots anchor them during storms, feed them nutrients from the soil, and help them grow. Without strong roots, even the tallest tree would be vulnerable to the first strong wind.

Your critical thinking skills need deep and sturdy roots as well—core habits and mindsets that nourish your ability to analyze, question, and make sound decisions. These habits act as a foundation, keeping you steady when faced with uncertainty, helping you extract valuable lessons from your experiences, and allowing you to grow into a sharper, more insightful thinker.

Like a tree that spreads its roots wide to access the best nutrients, a strong critical thinker continuously seeks new knowledge, challenges assumptions, and refines their perspective. By nurturing these foundational habits, you equip yourself to stand firm in the face of life's complexities, adapting and thriving no matter how the winds of change may blow.

Here are eight root habits that will help you to be a critical thinker and practical exercises to apply them in your daily life.

1. Curiosity

Always Ask Questions. Remember when you were little and constantly asked, "Why?" That natural curiosity is your first root habit. Strong critical thinkers:

- Stay curious about how things work
- Ask questions even when others don't
- Wonder about things others take for granted

- Get excited about learning new stuff

Try This: Pick something you use every day (like your phone or favorite snack) and ask five "How?" or "Why?" questions about it. You might be surprised by how little you know about familiar things!

2. Open-Mindedness

Keep Your Mind Flexible: Shasha and I decided to play a catching game. Occasionally, I tried to catch a ball with a closed fist, but it didn't work. My hand needs to be open, just like your mind. This means:

- Being willing to change your opinion when you learn new information

- Listening to ideas different from your own

- Admitting when you're wrong (yes, it's hard, but it makes you stronger!)

- Understanding that most issues aren't simply black and white

Challenge Yourself: Think of something you strongly believe. Now, try to list three reasons why someone might disagree with you. You don't have to change your mind; instead, understand other viewpoints.

3. Clarity

Clarity is about understanding the difference between facts, opinions, and assumptions. A strong foundation requires being honest with yourself about what you know and what you don't.

When you read or hear something, ask, "Is this a fact or an opinion?". You should also identify areas where your knowledge is incomplete and commit to learning more.

4. Critical Awareness

Awareness of your biases, emotions, and thought patterns is essential for thinking clearly. Just as a tree depends on the quality of its soil, your thinking relies on the quality of your awareness. To build awareness, reflect on your decisions and consider what influenced them. Notice when emotions cloud your judgment, and take a moment to pause before reacting.

5. Evidence-Based Thinking

Look for Proof. This root is super important in the age of social media and fake news. Good critical thinkers:

- Ask, "How do we know this is true?"
- Look for reliable sources
- Check facts before sharing information
- Understand the difference between facts and opinions

Real-Life Practice: Wait before sharing the next time you see a surprising social media post. Take five minutes to check if it's true. Where did the information come from? Can you find reliable sources saying the same thing?

6. Systematic Thinking

Have you ever tried to put together furniture without following the instructions? That usually doesn't end well! Systematic thinking means:

- Breaking big problems into smaller pieces
- Taking time to plan before acting
- Following logical steps

- Checking your work along the way

Try This Exercise: Pick a goal (like improving your grades or learning a new skill). Break it down into the smallest possible steps. Being systematic makes major challenges manageable!

7. Consistency

A tree doesn't grow overnight. It requires time and consistent care to develop deep roots. Similarly, critical thinking is a skill you develop through practice.

To practice consistency, set aside time each week to reflect on your thoughts and decisions and question your assumptions regularly.

8. Reflection

This might be the most potent root of all. Strong critical thinkers:

- Take time to think about their decisions
- Learn from mistakes
- Consider what worked and what didn't
- Apply past lessons to new situations
- Ask open-ended questions (what did I learn from this situation? What could I have done differently?
- Keep a thinking journal – write down your thoughts and observations. Over time, you'll notice patterns in your thinking and areas for improvement.
- Create a space for quiet – take time to sit quietly and let your thoughts settle.

Start Now: Keep a "Decision Journal" for a week. Write down one decision you make each day and why you made it. At the end of the week, look back – what patterns do you see?

Types of Questions for Critical Thinking

To become a skilled questioner, it's helpful to know the different types of questions and when to use them:

1. *Clarifying Questions* - These questions help you ensure you understand what was said. Example: "When you say the bird is endangered, what do you mean by that?"

2. *Probing Questions* - These go deeper, encouraging someone to explain or expand on their ideas. Example: "Why do you think this bird prefers nesting on the island instead of the shore?"

3. *Challenging Questions* - These invite someone to think critically about their assumptions or conclusions (but should be asked respectfully). Example: "You mentioned this area is the bird's natural habitat. Are there other places where it could thrive?"

4. *Reflective Questions* - These encourage introspection and self-awareness. Example: "How do you think your actions today affected the group dynamic?"

5. *Creative Questions* - These inspire new ways of thinking or imagining possibilities. Example: "If you could design the perfect habitat for this bird, what would it look like?"

Rooting Yourself in Strong Values

Nature teaches us that roots don't just hold a tree in place—they also provide nourishment and connection to the environment. Similarly, your mental foundation is strengthened by rooting yourself in strong values. Trees also prevent landslides so by applying critical thinking we also affect people around us positively. Let's explore some key values that support critical thinking:

1. *Honesty* - Being truthful with yourself and others ensures that your thinking is based on reality, not wishful thinking or deception.

2. *Humility* - Recognizing that you don't have all the answers opens the door to learning and growth. Your thinking becomes sharper when you admit what you don't know.

3. *Courage* - Critical thinking often means challenging popular opinions or stepping out of your comfort zone. Courage helps you stand firm in your convictions while remaining open to new ideas.

The Importance of Self-Belief

The ability to think critically begins with belief—belief in your ability to face challenges, create solutions, and carve your path. Often, the biggest obstacle to starting isn't external; it's the internal voice of doubt. Trust your instincts. The birds in the park know when to soar or when to nest; you too have an innate sense of direction. Keep trusting, even when the way forward isn't clear. Celebrate your strength. Everyone has unique abilities that equip them to tackle problems in their own way. Instead of comparing your experience to someone else's, focus on what you have.

During one of our visits, Shasha was apprehensive about climbing a steep section of the hill. I encouraged her to take it one step at a time and reminded her of the times she'd already climbed even more demanding paths. I encouraged and praised her for trying. With a mix of effort and belief in herself, she reached the top, beaming with pride. This moment was a reminder that belief is often the first step to achievement.

Believing in yourself means acknowledging that your experience will differ from anyone else's—and that's expected. Dare to be different and learn along the way. No two birds take the same route in the park, yet they all reach their destination. You don't have to follow a pre-defined path to find success; you can create one that aligns with your values, goals, and passions.

Overcoming Challenges to Building Strong Roots

Building a strong foundation isn't always easy. As you develop your roots, ensure that you avoid:

1. *Rushing*: Good thinking takes time. When you rush, you make mistakes and miss important details.

2. *The Fear of Being Wrong*: Everyone is wrong sometimes. Being wrong and learning from it makes your thinking stronger.

3. *Following the Crowd*: Just because "everyone" thinks something doesn't make it right. Your brain needs to do its thinking.

You may sometimes feel impatient, eager for instant results, but remember—true growth takes time. Strong roots take time to grow, but they're worth the effort. A towering oak doesn't sprout overnight, and neither will your critical thinking skills. Each new insight, each moment of reflection, adds another ring to the tree of your wisdom. Be patient with yourself. Every strong thinker was once a beginner, just as every mighty oak was once a fragile sapling.

At times, you may fear failure, worrying that a wrong turn or a mistaken assumption means you're not cut out for critical thinking. But consider this: when a tree's roots encounter a rock, they don't stop growing; they twist, stretch, and find another way. Obstacles are not the end of growth, they are part of the process. Instead of fearing failure, embrace it as a chance to refine your approach, adjust your perspective, and develop resilience.

You may also feel overwhelmed. In today's world, information floods in from every direction, and it can be hard to know where to start. But just as a tree draws nourishment from one root at a time, you, too, can focus on one idea, one question, one challenge at a time. Don't be afraid to seek guidance from mentors, books, or trusted sources. Critical thinking isn't a solitary journey—it thrives on discussion, curiosity, and the willingness to explore new pathways.

In the next chapter, we'll build on these foundations as we learn to see the bigger picture – the bird's eye view. But for now, focus on strengthening these essential habits; they'll support everything you know about critical thinking. As tree roots grow stronger with time and nurturing, your critical thinking foundations will develop with practice and patience.

Key Takeaways from Chapter 2

1. **Strong Foundation Supports Growth** – Just as tree roots anchor a tree, your critical thinking depends on building strong habits like curiosity, logic, and open-mindedness.

2. **Deep Roots Prevent You from Being Easily Swayed** – Without a solid foundation, your thinking can be influenced by misinformation, biases, or emotions, much like a shallow-rooted tree being uprooted by strong winds.

3. **Curiosity is the First Root of Critical Thinking** – Asking questions, wondering how things work, and challenging assumptions are essential habits that strengthen your ability to think critically.

4. **Reflection Strengthens Your Thinking** – Taking time to analyze past decisions, learn from mistakes, and recognize patterns in your thought process deepens your understanding and helps you make better choices.

5. **Root Yourself in Strong Values** – Honesty, humility, and courage provide a strong ethical foundation that ensures your thinking remains balanced and principled.

6. **Self-Belief is Key to Growth** – Just as trees grow despite obstacles, believing in your ability to learn and adapt helps you overcome challenges and develop resilience in your thinking.

7. **Growth Takes Time and Patience** – Developing strong critical thinking habits doesn't happen overnight. Like tree roots, they grow with consistent effort, reflection, and real-world practice.

EXERCISE

Here are five habits you can start today to strengthen your critical thinking roots:

1. **Ask at least one "Why?" question every day** – Whether it's a rule at school, a trending topic online, or something you hear in a conversation, take a moment to ask why.

2. **Read something challenging (not just social media!)** – Try reading an article, book, or essay that challenges your usual way of thinking.

3. **Talk to people who think differently from you** – Have thoughtful conversations with classmates, family members, or even online communities with diverse opinions.

4. **Take five minutes to reflect before making decisions** – Give yourself space to think things through rather than acting on impulse. Consider possible outcomes, weigh different options,

5. **Write down what you learn from mistakes** – By reflecting on your mistakes, you turn them into stepping stones for growth rather than roadblocks.

PART II

Observing, Analyzing, & Understanding

It's better to run with winners and lose than to run with losers and win.

—Andrea Campbell

Chapter Three

A Bird's Eye View: Seeing the Bigger Picture

There's something transformative about elevation. When you rise above the ground and view the world from a higher vantage point, the ordinary becomes extraordinary. You see not just the individual parts of the puzzle but also how they fit together. What once seemed chaotic and confusing reveals intricate patterns of life that make sense.

The Transformative Power of Elevation

During our walk in the reserve, we climbed a stony hill leading to the area's highest point. From there, the lake spread below us, its calm waters reflecting the sky. Beyond the reserve's borders, the city skyline emerged in the distance, its towers standing tall like sentinels of progress.

Although these towers were miles away, they felt within reach from this height. This moment imparted a powerful lesson: when we rise higher, we can see further. It's not just about physical distance; it represents a shift in perspective.

What seemed overwhelming or unclear from the ground can become manageable and interconnected from above. This is the essence of gaining a bird's-eye view, a critical component of becoming a thoughtful, strategic thinker. It's a powerful tool that empowers you to take control and make confident decisions.

Why the Bigger Picture Matters

Focusing on the bigger picture allows you to:

1. *Understand Context*: Seeing the larger framework helps you recognize how individual elements interact and influence each other, revealing connections others might miss.

2. *Prioritize Effectively*: When you know what truly matters, you can make more informed decisions and focus your energy where it counts.

3. *Anticipate Outcomes*: A broader perspective helps you foresee potential challenges and opportunities.

The Interplay of Perspective in Nature

Nature offers some of the best lessons in perspective-taking. Consider a tree in the reserve. At first glance, it's just one of many trees blending into the landscape. But upon closer inspection, you notice its unique features: the texture of its bark, the shape of its leaves, and the creatures it supports—birds nesting in its branches, ants marching along its trunk, and moss clinging to its roots.

Now, imagine you're a bird soaring above the park. From this vantage point, the tree is part of a vast ecosystem: it produces oxygen, provides shade, and connects with countless other trees through underground networks. Both perspectives—the intimate details and the sweeping panorama—are essential for understanding the tree's role in the ecosystem.

Birds assemble and fly over the reserve

The View from Above

Birds often symbolize freedom and vision. They soar high above the world, observing landscapes in their entirety. A heron flying over the reserve doesn't just see a single tree or the lake; it perceives the entire ecosystem.

We can emulate this by learning to "fly" above our problems and situations, gaining clarity that comes only from a broader view. Had we focused solely on the stony hill's gravel underfoot as we climbed, we'd have missed the beauty of the surrounding landscape, the thrill of reaching the summit, and the lessons waiting at the top.

The climb itself is part of the process. We had to navigate uneven terrain to reach the peak, which brought some discomfort. In the same way, gaining perspective often requires effort and persistence and can be uncomfortable. But the reward, the ability to see further and understand more, is always worth it.

The Components of a Birds-Eye View

To develop the habit of seeing the bigger picture, consider these three elements:

1. *Context*: Understanding the environment or situation is the first step. Ask yourself: What's the broader purpose or goal? How do individual parts connect to the whole?

For instance, in a family argument, the immediate disagreement might be about chores, but the bigger picture could involve feelings of being unappreciated or overburdened. Recognizing this allows you to address the real issue. Similarly, in a school group project, focusing on the bigger picture could mean understanding the project's impact on the group's goals, rather than just completing your assigned tasks.

2. *Patterns*: A higher perspective reveals patterns and trends that aren't visible at ground level. What recurring themes or behaviors do you notice? Are there connections you haven't seen before?

Looking at your school performance, for example, a bird's-eye view might reveal that your struggles with deadlines are linked to procrastination rather than ability.

3. *Prioritization*: When you see the bigger picture, you can better identify what's truly important. What demands immediate attention? What can wait?

This skill is particularly valuable when balancing multiple responsibilities, such as schoolwork, extracurricular activities, and family commitments.

Techniques to See the Bigger Picture

1. Climb Higher (Literally or Figuratively)

In the same way that Shasha and I climbed the hill, you can take steps to gain a better vantage point:

- *Physically*: Go to a place that offers a broad view, like a park, hill, or rooftop. Let the expansive view inspire you to think more broadly about your life.

- *Mentally*: Take a step back from a problem. Give yourself time and space to reflect before diving into solutions.

2. Use Visualization

Create a mental or physical map of a situation. For example:

- Sketch out a diagram of a problem, with its causes and effects.

- Write a timeline of events to see how they connect.

Visualization helps you organize your thoughts and identify missing pieces.

3. Seek Outside Perspectives

Ask others for their viewpoints. They might see connections or implications you've overlooked. For example, a friend might notice a pattern in your behavior that you hadn't realized, or a teacher might suggest a solution you hadn't considered.

4. Practice Reflective Thinking

After deciding or completing a project, reflect on how it fits your larger goals. What went well? What could you improve?

Tools for Getting Above the Trees

1. The Zoom Tool - Practice zooming in to look at details and out to see the whole picture. Find balance by connecting details to the big picture.

For example, Social Media Use

- Zoom In: Individual posts and interactions
- Zoom Out: Consider the overall impact on society
- Balance: How your usage affects your life goals

2. The Connection Compass - Ask these questions:

- What's connected to this?
- Who's affected?
- What systems are involved?
- What might change because of this?

3. The Time Telescope – Look across different time frames:

- How did this start?

- What's changing now?
- Where is this heading?
- What patterns repeat?

Common Altitude Errors

1. Ground-Level Thinking

Problem: Getting stuck in details.

Solution: Regular "elevation checks" – step back and look at the whole situation

2. Clouded Vision

Problem: Letting emotions block the bigger picture

Solution: The CLEAR method:

- Check your emotional state
- List all factors involved
- Examine connections
- Analyze patterns
- Review from different angles

3. Tunnel Vision

Problem: Focusing on only one aspect

Solution: The 360° Scan:

- Look in all directions
- Consider multiple factors

- Check blind spots

Real-Life Applications of Seeing the Bigger Picture

1. In Problem-Solving

When faced with a challenge, stepping back to see its broader context often reveals solutions. For example, if a classmate is acting distant, considering their overall behavior and circumstances—rather than just their recent actions—might provide insight into their feelings.

2. In Decision-Making

Decisions made in isolation can have unintended consequences. Taking the bigger picture into account ensures your choices align with your long-term goals. It helps to consider long-term impacts, look at effects on others, and consider wider consequences.

3. In Relationships

Understanding the bigger picture in relationships helps you navigate conflicts and foster deeper connections. For example, seeing a sibling's frustrations as part of their broader struggles can lead to empathy and constructive support.

Towers on the Horizon

The towers of the city we saw from the top of the stony hill symbolized possibility, progress, and perspective. What had seemed distant and abstract from the ground became tangible and real from our higher vantage point.

The same principle applies to life. The further you climb, whether through education, self-reflection, or experiences, the more you can see. And as your perspective expands, so does your understanding of the world and your place within it.

The bird's eye view isn't just a way of thinking; it's a way of living. It's about rising above the immediate, the mundane, and the myopic to grasp the profound interconnectedness of life. And in doing so, you'll not only see further; you'll also soar higher.

Learning from Birds: Adaptability and Focus

Birds in flight often adjust their altitude based on their needs. When hunting, a hawk swoops low to focus on its prey. It flies high to conserve energy and see the broader landscape when migrating. Similarly, your ability to shift perspectives—zooming in when necessary and zooming out when appropriate—is a skill worth mastering.

When Developing this Skill, ask Yourself the Right Questions. When stuck in the details, ask, "What's the bigger picture here?" When overwhelmed by the big picture, ask, "What specific step can I take now?" Regularly remind yourself to step back and evaluate situations from a broader perspective. Reflect on past situations where gaining perspective helped you make better decisions.

As you cultivate the habit of seeing the bigger picture, you'll develop tools and techniques that make this skill second nature. These include:

• *Mind Mapping*: Create visual representations of your thoughts and ideas to see connections more clearly.

• *Journaling*: Writing about your experiences helps you process them and identify patterns over time.

• *Seeking Feedback*: Others often have perspectives we can't see. Be proactive in asking for their insights.

Flying Higher Together

As we descended the hill that day, the city towers still in view, I realized that the climb wasn't just about the view; it was about the course we travelled to reach it. Every step up the stony hill and every moment of effort contributed to the clarity and wonder we felt at the top.

Gaining a bird's eye view isn't a solitary endeavor. Surround yourself with people who encourage you to see beyond your immediate challenges. Together, you can soar higher and achieve more than you ever thought possible.

Let this chapter inspire you to climb your hills, literally or metaphorically, and embrace the broader horizons that come into view. A vast, interconnected world awaits you to explore, understand, and contribute to. Like a bird learning to fly, getting the bigger picture takes practice. Start with small situations and gradually tackle more complex ones. The view from above is worth the effort!

Now that you've explored the power of perspective, you're ready to delve into the next chapter, which will help you recognize reliable sources as you process information. Each step builds on the last, like climbing a hill to reach a breathtaking view. Let's continue this path with our eyes wide open, ready to embrace the broader horizons that await one thoughtful step at a time.

Key Takeaways from Chapter 3

1. **Elevation Transforms Perspective** – Gaining a higher vantage point helps turn confusion into clarity. Problems that seem overwhelming at ground level

often reveal patterns and solutions when viewed from above.

2. **Seeing the Bigger Picture Enhances Decision-Making** – A broader perspective allows you to understand context, anticipate outcomes, and prioritize effectively. This prevents you from getting stuck in minor details and helps you focus on what truly matters.

3. **Nature Teaches Us About Perspective** – Just like a bird soaring over a landscape sees connections that aren't visible from the ground, we can train ourselves to step back and recognize the relationships between different elements in our lives.

4. **Perspective-Taking Requires Effort** – Just as climbing a hill takes energy and persistence, shifting your mindset to see the bigger picture isn't always easy. It requires patience, reflection, and the willingness to step outside your immediate concerns.

5. **Balance Between Detail and Big Picture is Key** – A skilled thinker knows when to zoom in on details and when to zoom out for a broader view. Like a bird adjusting its altitude, being adaptable in your perspective strengthens problem-solving and strategic thinking.

6. **Practical Techniques Help Develop a Bird's Eye View** – Methods like visualization, asking the right questions, and seeking feedback allow you to train your mind to see patterns, recognize trends, and connect ideas more effectively.

7. **Soaring Higher is part of a Journey, Not a Destination** – Expanding your perspective is a lifelong process. The more you challenge yourself

to rise above the immediate, the clearer your understanding becomes, allowing you to navigate life with greater wisdom and insight.

Exercise

1. **Choose a Current Challenge:** Identify a situation where you feel stuck.

2. **Zoom Out:** Ask yourself, "What's the broader context? How does this fit into my overall goals or values?"

3. **Find Patterns:** Reflect on whether this challenge is part of a more significant trend in your life.

4. **Prioritize:** Determine what aspect of the situation deserves your attention first.

5. **Act:** Use the insights you've gained to take thoughtful steps forward.

Chapter Four

Barking Up the Wrong Tree: Recognizing Reliable Sources

We noticed that every tree in the park was different. Some are strong and reliable; others look weak or dying. When looking for information, sources are like trees – some are sturdy and trustworthy, while others might collapse under closer inspection.

In the dense forest of information we encounter daily, it's easy to find ourselves barking up the wrong tree—investing time and energy into unreliable sources or misleading ideas. In today's world of social media, viral posts, and fake news, knowing how to find reliable sources is more important than ever.

To become a critical thinker, you must learn to discern which trees are worth climbing and which are hollow. This chapter will guide you through the skills needed to recognize reliable sources, an essential step for making informed decisions and forming sound judgments.

Understanding Information Overload

In today's world, we are bombarded with information from every direction. Social media, news outlets, online forums, conversations, and advertisements compete for our attention, which can sometimes feel overwhelming. It's like standing in the middle of the park, surrounded by dozens of paths, not knowing which one to take.

Critical thinking will help you to analyze information effectively and make more informed choices.

Imagine being given a map of the nature reserve without clear markers or signs. You might see many paths, but making a confident decision without knowing which leads to your desired destination would be hard. Similarly, when we face an overload of information, we often don't know where to begin. The key is to focus on what's relevant and filter out the noise.

Squirrel hiding in a tree as dogs pass by

The Importance of Reliable Sources

Every decision, belief, or conclusion you reach relies on the information you have. But what happens when the information is incorrect, biased, or incomplete? Trusting unreliable sources can lead to poor decisions, wasted effort, and harm.

Imagine you're planning a picnic at the park, and you check the weather forecast. If you rely on an unreliable app that inaccurately predicts clear skies, you might get caught in a rainstorm. Similarly, reliable information is the foundation of success in more significant areas of life—like career decisions, relationships, or health.

The TREES Method for Checking Sources

Would you build a treehouse in a dead tree or rely on a broken branch to hold your weight? Similarly, you wouldn't pick a berry in the forest and eat it if you were not sure it was safe. Using unreliable information can lead to bad decisions and the spread of false information. It spoils your reputation and causes you to miss opportunities. You may even cause harm to yourself or others.

By mastering the TREES method, you will gain the confidence to identify trustworthy sources. This method, inspired by the spirit of the forest, provides key indicators to look for, empowering you to handle the information landscape with ease.

T - Trustworthy: Ask yourself, who created this information? What are their credentials? Do they have expertise in this area? What's their reputation? Conduct a quick check by looking up the author or organization to see what other reliable sources say about them. Do they have the expertise, qualifications, or experience to speak on the subject? For example, if you're learning about swans at the nature reserve, a wildlife biologist would be a more reliable source than someone casually passing by.

R – Recent: Ascertain if the information is still relevant today and if anything has changed. Is the information applicable to your situation? Does it address your specific questions or needs?

Outdated sources or generalizations may not provide the nuanced insights you need. For instance, a study from decades ago about bird migration patterns may no longer reflect modern findings. Some topics need very recent sources (like technology), while others can use older sources (like historical events).

E - Evidence: Look for facts and statistics from primary sources, expert opinions, scientific research, citations, and references. Accurate sources cite their evidence clearly, allowing you to cross-check the information. Be cautious of vague or unsubstantiated statements, like "Everyone knows this is true," without proof.

Watch out for red flags such as "people say...," "Studies show..." (without naming the studies), "Everyone knows..." and claims that seem too good to be true.

E – Elsewhere: Do multiple independent sources corroborate the facts? Check if other reliable sources say the same thing and if the information can be verified. Check for different viewpoints and see if experts agree or disagree. When you find information, look for at least two other reliable sources that confirm it. Trustworthy information often aligns with established knowledge. If a single source claims something radically different without evidence, approach it cautiously.

S – Slant: Consider the purpose of the information. Are they trying to sell something? Is the information presented objectively or skewed to favor a particular perspective? Could there be hidden agendas, and is there evidence of bias? Recognizing bias helps you separate fact from persuasion. Bias isn't always obvious. A food company promoting a "scientific study" that praises its products is likely presenting biased information.

Recognizing bias helps you separate fact from persuasion. Being alert to such tactics helps you maintain a vigilant stance when evaluating sources.

The Source Reliability Spectrum

Most Reliable (Well-documented, reviewed & fact-checked)

- University research (e.g. peer-reviewed journals)
- International organizations (e.g., WHO, UN, IMF)
- Historical archives (primary source documents, official records)
- Official government data (government web pages)
- Established scientific organizations
- Well-known, reputable news organizations
- Expert books and publications

Sometimes Reliable (Needs verification & cross-checking)

- News websites (e.g., opinion pieces or breaking news)
- Personal expert blogs (check credentials are legitimate)
- Company websites (may be biased toward their products and services)

- Documentary films (may have a specific agenda)
- Wikipedia (use as a starting point, but verify cited sources)
- Social media posts by experts (check link to primary sources)

Least Reliable (Often opinion-based or misleading)

- Clickbait websites (sensationalist headlines with exaggerated claims and little credible sourcing)
- Satire or parody sites (often meant to be humorous)
- Random social media posts that lack proof
- Unverified forums and message boards (e.g., Reddit, Quora, unless sourced)
- Conspiracy theory websites (promote misinformation and pseudoscience)
- Chain messages
- Personal opinions that lack proof
- Sites with lots of ads and pop-ups
- Websites without an author name or citations

Recognizing Patterns in Reliable Information

Recognizing patterns in reliable information can provide a sense of security. Just as experienced hikers learn to recognize the well-trodden paths that lead them safely through the forest, critical thinkers develop the ability to spot patterns in reliable information. These patterns act as guideposts, helping you make your way through the vast and sometimes confusing landscape of facts, opinions, and arguments.

Trustworthy sources don't just make claims—they exhibit consistency in their presentation, tone, and transparency. They provide evidence to back up their assertions, cite reputable references, and acknowledge multiple perspectives. Their language is measured, not sensationalized, and they welcome scrutiny rather than avoiding it. Over time, you'll notice that reliable information has a rhythm—a steady, reasoned quality that reassures you of its credibility, much like the familiar and steady rustling of leaves in a trusted old oak.

By sharpening your ability to recognize these patterns, you build a sense of security in your knowledge. You become less susceptible to misinformation and more confident in your ability to sift through the noise. The roots of a tree instinctively find water and nutrients; similarly, your critical thinking skills will lead you toward deeper understanding and well-founded conclusions.

Characteristics of Reliable Sources

1. *Clear Intentions*: Trustworthy sources aim to inform rather than manipulate. They avoid sensationalism and focus on presenting facts.

2. *Transparent Methods*: Reliable sources explain how they arrived at their conclusions. For example, a scientific study will outline its methodology, sample size, and limitations.

3. *Professional Tone*: A reliable source communicates professionally and avoids inflammatory language.

4. *Responsibility and Accountability*: Credible sources are willing to issue corrections or updates when they've made errors.

Building Familiarity with Trusted Sources

As you practice evaluating sources, you'll naturally build a repertoire of trusted names and platforms. For example:

- In health and science: The World Health Organization (WHO) or National Geographic.

- For academic research: Google Scholar or university libraries.

- For general news: Established publications with a history of fact-checking, like The Guardian or The New York Times

Common Pitfalls in Evaluating Sources

Even experienced critical thinkers can fall into traps when assessing information. Here are some common pitfalls to watch out for:

1. *Relying on Popular Opinion* – This is The Popular Fallacy that assumes that "If lots of people share it, it must be true." But popularity doesn't equal accuracy. Just because many people believe something doesn't make it accurate. Herd mentality can lead to widespread acceptance of misinformation.

2. *Trusting Sources Based on Emotion* - Emotionally charged stories or messages can be persuasive, but they may not be grounded in fact. While emotions are valid, they shouldn't dictate the credibility of information.

3. *Falling for Pseudo-Experts* - The Authority Trap assumes: "They look professional, so they must be right." Check credentials and evidence, not just appearance. Some sources appear authoritative but lack genuine expertise. Always verify credentials and cross-check their claims.

4. *Ignoring Context* - Information taken out of context can be misleading. Look at the broader picture to understand the whole meaning and implications.

5. *Personal Bias* – This is the Comfort Zone Error that assumes: "It agrees with what I think, so it must be true." Instead, be especially careful with information you want to believe.

Developing Information Literacy

Information literacy is finding, evaluating, and using information effectively. Building this skill set involves:

1. *Practicing Skepticism*: Healthy skepticism doesn't mean doubting everything—it means questioning sources until they prove their reliability.

2. *Conducting Independent Research*: Instead of accepting information at face value, dig deeper. Read articles, consult experts, and compare viewpoints.

3. *Using Credible Resources*: Look for reputable websites, libraries, and academic journals. Avoid sources known for sensationalism or bias.

4. *Teaching Yourself to Pause*: Forming opinions quickly in our fast-paced world is tempting. Take a moment to pause, reflect, and evaluate the information thoroughly.

Real-World Applications

1. *In School* - Consider how you choose sources for assignments, where to find reliable research, and how to cite sources. Consider also when to question information.

Imagine you're writing a report about climate change. Relying on unreliable sources could spread misinformation, weaken your argument, and reduce your grade. Your work will have a significant impact by prioritizing scientific research and credible organizations.

2. *In Social Media* - Social media is a hotbed of misinformation. Before sharing a post, ask yourself: Is this from a reliable source? Could it be misleading or out of context? Consider how to spot fake news, share information, and fact-check claims. What will you do about misinformation?

3. *In Everyday Decisions* - Reliable information ensures better decisions, from choosing a healthcare provider to buying a new gadget. Look for reviews, expert opinions, and verified facts before committing.

Avoiding unreliable sources is essential not just for formal research or academic work but for everyday decision-making. Whether you're evaluating news articles, social media posts, product reviews, or even advice from friends, distinguishing between credible information and misinformation shapes your understanding of the world. The ability to filter out unreliable sources protects you from being misled, helps you make informed choices, and strengthens your ability to think critically in every aspect of life. Here are a few everyday contexts where this skill is vital:

1. *Shopping Decisions* - When making significant purchases, such as a laptop or a car, it's easy to be swayed by advertisements or biased reviews. Instead, consult independent review platforms and compare features across multiple sources to make an informed choice.

2. *Personal Advice* - We often turn to friends or family for advice, but even well-meaning loved ones can share outdated or inaccurate information. Evaluate their advice based on its alignment with credible evidence or seek second opinions when necessary.

3. *Online Communities* - People frequently share opinions disguised as facts in forums or social media groups. Before taking their advice, establish: Who are these people? What's their expertise? Is there evidence to support their claims?

Interim Reflection Exercise: Evaluating Sources

1. Identify a Source: Choose information you've recently encountered, such as a news article, social media post, or conversation.

2. Apply the 5 Criteria: The TREES Method for checking sources.

3. Decide Its reliability: Is this a worthy source? Why or why not?

What Happens When You Bark Up the Wrong Tree?

Learning to recognize reliable sources takes time and practice. Mistakes are inevitable, but each misstep brings you closer to becoming a more discerning thinker. By developing this skill, you'll protect yourself from misinformation and empower yourself to make confident, informed choices in every aspect of life.

The consequences of trusting unreliable sources can range from minor inconveniences to significant setbacks. Let's explore some scenarios:

Case Study 1: The Nutrition Myth

Imagine someone trying to lose weight by following a trendy diet they read about online. The source claims that cutting out an entire food group is the key to success, but it lacks scientific backing. Trusting this source could lead to nutritional deficiencies, frustration, and wasted effort.

Case Study 2: The Misguided Debate

A student uses unverified statistics from a biased blog in a school debate to argue their point. The opposing team quickly identifies the flaw, weakening the student's credibility and their overall argument.

These examples show how barking up the wrong tree—placing trust in unreliable sources—can undermine your goals and confidence. So, the next time you encounter new information, take a moment to evaluate it critically. With each tree you choose wisely, your critical thinking skills will strengthen, setting the stage for success in the chapters and challenges ahead.

A Final Word on Avoiding Misinformation

Recognizing reliable sources is an ongoing process. It requires curiosity, skepticism, and the courage to challenge your assumptions. When you approach information with this mindset, you empower yourself to make choices based on truth and insight rather than deception or guesswork.

The next time you encounter new information, pause and think: Is this tree worth climbing? Avoiding the wrong ones will save time, energy, and mental clarity for the trees that genuinely matter.

In the next chapter, "Digital Pathways: Navigating Online Information," we'll dive deeper into how to navigate the digital world and make sense of online information. Let's keep climbing, one branch of reliable knowledge at a time.

Key Takeaways from Chapter 4

1. **Not All Sources Are Equal** – Just as trees in a park vary in strength, sources of information differ in reliability. Some are sturdy and trustworthy, while others are weak or misleading. Critical thinking requires learning to recognize the difference.

2. **Use the TREES framework for Evaluating Sources**: **T**rustworthy (Verify the creator's credentials and expertise); **R**ecent (Check if the information is up to date and relevant); **E**vidence (Look for citations, research, and factual backing); **E**lsewhere (Cross-check with multiple reliable sources); **S**lant (Identify bias or hidden agendas behind the information).

3. **Recognizing Reliable vs. Unreliable Sources** – Peer-reviewed journals, government data, and major news organizations are typically reliable, while anonymous social media posts, clickbait, and opinion-based sources require scrutiny.

4. **Common Pitfalls in Evaluating Information** – Avoid traps such as trusting popular opinion, being swayed by emotional arguments, believing pseudo-experts, and ignoring context. Personal biases can also cloud judgment.

5. **Building Information Literacy** – Develop skills like skepticism, independent research, using credible resources, and pausing before forming conclusions. These habits help navigate the overwhelming amount of daily information.

6. **Real-World Applications of Reliable Information** – Fact-checking is essential in academics, social

media, personal decisions, and even shopping. Choosing credible sources prevents misinformation from influencing critical choices.

7. **The Consequences of Misinformation** – Trusting unreliable sources can lead to bad decisions, lost credibility, and wasted effort.

Reflection Exercise:

Build Your Source Radar

To strengthen your ability to identify reliable sources, try this:

1. **Choose a Topic:** Select a topic you're curious about, such as climate change, nutrition, or a recent news event.

2. **Gather Information:** Find three different sources discussing the topic.

3. **Evaluate the Sources**:

- Who published it?

- Are there citations or supporting evidence?

- Does the information align with what other credible sources are saying?

4. **Rate Their Reliability:** Assign a score (1-5) to each source based on its credibility, with 5 being highly reliable.

5. **Reflect:** What patterns did you notice? Which sources stood out as trustworthy?

Chapter Five

Seeing the Wood for the Trees: Gaining Perspective

In life, as in nature, our view of the world often depends on where we're standing. Sometimes, we get so focused on a single tree—one problem, one moment, or one detail—that we fail to see the vast forest surrounding it. Other times, we see the forest but miss the richness of the individual trees. Critical thinking requires balancing both perspectives: the big picture and the finer details. This chapter will guide you in developing the ability to shift perspectives, an essential skill for understanding complex situations and making informed decisions.

As we strolled, we noticed a swan near the lake. Had we focused solely on the swan, we might have missed the heron perched gracefully on a nearby tree or the way the sunlight penetrated the dense forest and danced on the water. Conversely, if we're only admiring the beauty of the entire scene, we might fail to notice that the swan's wing is injured.

Imagine standing so close to a tree that your nose touches its bark. You can see every tiny detail—each crack, each bit of moss, maybe even some small insects. But can you tell what kind of forest you're in? Or where the nearest stream is? Or which way leads home? Sometimes, we get so focused on small details that we lose sight of the whole picture. Stepping back allows you to see not just one tree, but the entire landscape—how everything connects, how the paths wind, and where they might lead.

Fallen tree still thrives - change your perspective

In critical thinking, seeing the wood for the trees involves recognizing the interplay between the parts and the whole. It's about not getting lost in the details (the trees) and being able to step back and see the entire situation (the wood).

Seeing the wood for the trees means understanding how individual parts contribute to the whole and recognizing the broader context. Finding the right balance is crucial for understanding complex issues and making informed decisions. This balance guides us, ensuring that no detail is overlooked and no larger context is ignored, giving us the confidence that we are considering all aspects of a situation.

Why Details Can Be Deceptive

Have you ever spent hours studying for a test by memorizing every fact, only to realize you don't understand how everything fits together? Or have you gotten so caught up in a social media argument about a tiny point that you forgot the original discussion? Welcome to the "trees versus forest" problem.

Details can be important, but they can also be deceptive. They can distract, overwhelm, or even mislead us if we don't step back and consider the full context. A single tree doesn't define an entire forest; similarly, one piece of information rarely tells the whole story.

Critical thinking requires zooming in when necessary but also stepping back to see how everything fits together. The challenge is learning when to focus on the details and when to shift your perspective to grasp the bigger picture.

Sometimes we fall into what we'll call the "Detail Trap"

- Obsessing over individual facts without understanding their context.
- Missing important patterns because we're too zoomed in.
- Losing track of our main goals while chasing minor points.
- Getting overwhelmed by information instead of seeing the story it tells.

Gaining Perspective

Gaining perspective allows us to:

- Avoid Misjudgment: Considering all angles reduces the risk of jumping to conclusions based on incomplete information.

- Enhance Creativity: A broader perspective opens our minds to new possibilities and solutions.

- Foster Empathy: Seeing things from other people's viewpoints helps us understand their feelings and motivations.

For example, focusing only on your contribution might make you feel underappreciated when analyzing a school project. But taking a step back to see the entire team's efforts can help you appreciate the collective achievement and your role.

Techniques for Gaining Perspective

1. Step Back Physically and Mentally

When immersed in a situation, it's easy to lose sight of the bigger picture. Physically stepping back—like taking a walk, as Shasha and I do at the reserve—can provide mental clarity. Reflecting on the broader context often reveals insights you might have missed.

For example, if you're frustrated about losing a soccer match, taking a step back might reveal a bigger picture—you didn't just play a game; you built teamwork, tested your resilience, and gained valuable lessons from mistakes. Every setback holds an opportunity for growth if you're willing to look beyond the immediate disappointment.

2. Practice "Zooming In" and "Zooming Out"

Critical thinkers toggle between zooming in to focus on details and zooming out to grasp the bigger picture.

- **Zooming In:** When you zoom in, you pay attention to specifics, like the data in a report or the unique features of a bird in the park.
- **Zooming Out:** When you zoom out, you connect those details to broader themes, like the purpose of the report or the ecosystem the bird belongs to.

Balancing these perspectives ensures no detail is overlooked and no larger context is ignored.

3. Adopt Multiple Viewpoints

Imagine standing in different spots around the lake. From one angle, you see the island clearly; from another, the city skyline dominates the view. Similarly, in critical thinking, adopting different viewpoints helps you understand the same situation from various angles.

For instance, in a disagreement, try to see the situation from the other person's perspective. What are their priorities? What might they be feeling?

4. Use the "5 Whys" Technique

Have you ever wondered why problems sometimes keep coming back, no matter how many times you try to fix them? That's because we often address only the symptoms rather than the root cause. The **"5 Whys"** technique is a simple but powerful tool that helps you dig deeper, moving from surface-level thinking to deeper understanding..

Start by asking "Why?" about a situation. Then, take the answer and ask **"Why?"** again. Repeat this at least five times, each time peeling back another layer of understanding. Like tracing a tree's roots beneath the soil, this process helps you move beyond surface-level thinking and get to the heart of the problem.

For example, if a student struggles with completing homework, the first "*Why?*" might reveal that they find it too difficult. Asking "*Why?*" again might uncover that they don't understand the material. Another "*Why?*" could show they missed a key lesson in class. By the time you reach the fifth "*Why?*", you might discover that the real issue is a lack of study strategies, not just a difficult assignment.

By identifying the true cause, you can develop solutions that actually work, rather than just treating the symptoms. Whether solving personal challenges or tackling big problems in the world, mastering the "5 Whys" technique sharpens your ability to think critically, make better decisions, and create lasting solutions.

An example from the nature reserve:

- Why is the swan acting aggressively?
- Because people are feeding it bread.
- Why is bread a problem?
- Because it's not part of their natural diet and causes health issues.
- Why do people feed bread to swans?
- Because they think it's helpful.
- Why do they think that?
- Because they don't know the risks.

5. Use Visual Tools

Diagrams, flowcharts, and maps can help you organize information and see connections. For example, creating a mind map of a problem allows you to visualize how its parts interact, making it easier to spot patterns and gaps.

Real-Life Applications

1. Problem-Solving in School

When solving problems, gaining perspective helps you identify causes, explore alternatives, and anticipate outcomes. Instead of just memorizing dates for history class, ask:

- What considerable changes were happening in this period?
- How did different events influence each other?
- What patterns keep repeating through history?
- What lessons can we apply from history to current events?
- How might the story change if told from another perspective?
- What were the unintended consequences of these events?

2. Conflict Resolution in Relationships

In conflicts, perspective-taking fosters understanding and cooperation. For example, when two friends argue over a misunderstanding, stepping back to see both sides can help them find common ground. When dealing with conflicts, consider:

- Is this argument about what we think it's about?
- What's the bigger picture of our relationship?
- Will this matter in a week? A month? A year?

3. In Decision Making and Goal Setting

Perspective helps you prioritize short-term actions within long-term plans. For instance, if you're saving for a trip, understanding the importance of small sacrifices (like skipping daily coffee purchases) in the context of the bigger goal keeps you motivated. Before making choices, think:

- How does this fit into my longer-term goals?
- What broader impacts might this decision have?
- Am I getting distracted by less important factors?

The Wood and the Trees in Everyday Life

Life constantly asks us to balance the woods and the trees, the grand view, and the intricate details. Whether you're planning your future, managing a conflict, or enjoying a walk in the park, your ability to shift perspectives is a tool that will serve you well.

Neither perspective is inherently better; it's about knowing when to focus and step back. Mastering this balance will make you a better thinker and enrich your experiences and relationships.

Sometimes, you need to focus on the bark of the tree—the details matter! But regularly stepping back to see the whole forest helps you make better decisions and understand complex situations. Stay focused on what's important and avoid getting lost in the details. The trick isn't choosing between minor details and the big picture, it's learning to dance between them.

Like a photographer who keeps adjusting their lens, you need to zoom in to understand specifics, zoom out to see the context and find the proper focus for each situation.

Key Takeaways from Chapter 5

1. **Balance Perspectives**: Critical thinking requires balancing detailed analysis (the trees) with holistic understanding (the wood) to develop a complete understanding of situations.

2. **Avoid the Detail Trap**: Focusing too much on isolated facts can lead to missing important patterns, losing sight of main goals, and becoming overwhelmed by information without understanding its significance.

3. **Perspective Enhances Decision-Making**: Gaining perspective helps avoid misjudgment, enhances creativity, and fosters empathy by allowing us to see situations from multiple viewpoints.

4. **Practice Zooming In and Out**: Effective critical thinkers can toggle between examining specific details (zooming in) and connecting those details to broader themes (zooming out).

5. **Use Structured Techniques**: Methods like the "5 Whys" technique and visual tools (diagrams, flowcharts, mind maps) help organize information and uncover root causes of problems.

6. **Apply Perspective in Daily Life**: This skill has practical applications in problem-solving, conflict resolution, and decision-making by helping identify causes, explore alternatives, and anticipate outcomes.

7. **Neither Perspective is Superior**: The chapter emphasizes that neither detailed focus nor big-picture thinking is inherently better—the key is knowing when to apply each perspective and how to shift between them appropriately.

Practice Exercises

1. **The News Challenge** - Take a news story and practice identifying the specific details (trees), the broader implications (woods) and how they connect.

2. **The Homework Perspective** - Next time you have a big assignment list all the small tasks involved, identify the main learning goals and connect how each task serves the goals.

Discussion Questions

1. When was the last time you got lost in the details? What helped you see the bigger picture?

2. How do you balance focusing on details with keeping the end goal in mind?

3. What situations in your life need a "zoom-out" right now?

4. How can you help others when they're too focused on the trees to see the forest?

Chapter Six

Finding the Right Track: Analyzing Information Effectively

One afternoon, we arrived at the park for our daily walk and noticed something new—several signs at the edge of the lake with bold letters warning visitors: **DO NOT FEED THE BIRDS!** The signs were a surprise because, for as long as we could remember, people had routinely tossed bits of bread into the lake and watched as ducks and geese eagerly pecked at the floating crumbs. But now, the park has changed its stance.

Feeding the birds, once seen as a kind gesture, had been harmful. We knew that there had been some issues some years before when several birds perished and the reserve was closed to vehicular traffic. We were never told exactly what happened but now, the sign made it clear: those who ignored the rule could face fines.

Analyzing Information & Staying Safe Online

This moment got me thinking about how information changes over time. What we once assumed to be correct may later be proven wrong. The same applies to the digital world, where new research, updated policies, and fact-checking constantly shape what we believe to be true. In the same way that we needed to adjust our understanding of the 'friendly' act of feeding birds, we also need to be flexible in assessing online information.

Today's world is bombarded with information from all directions—social media, news sites, friends, and even random internet searches. Finding the right track means analyzing this information effectively, separating facts from fiction, and making informed decisions. Just as a nature trail can have misleading paths that take you in the wrong direction, the digital world is filled with distractions, misinformation, and potential dangers. Critical thinking helps us stay on course.

Trusting the Right Signs

Signs exist to help people make informed choices. They offer guidance, prevent harm, and ensure the safety of everyone in a shared space. But what if trusted park rangers didn't put up the signs? What if someone made a sign, claiming: **"The lake is safe for swimming!"** Would you trust it? Would you jump in without question? Probably not. You'd likely look for confirmation—perhaps checking the official park rules, asking a ranger, or observing the water for danger signs like algae or strong currents.

Now, think of the internet as a massive park filled with millions of signs—some official and reliable, others misleading or completely false. How do you know which ones to trust? Before accepting something as accurate, ask: *Who put up this sign? Are they an expert? What's their motive?* Like in the park, online information should be verified before you follow it. Reliable sources are like official park signs. They exist to guide you in the right direction.

Shasha follows a beaten track

The Risk of Shortcut Trails

Throughout the nature reserve, there are shortcut trails where people have veered off the designated paths, wearing down the grass to create new routes. These shortcuts might seem like a good idea at first. After all, they lead to key areas more quickly. But over time, they cause damage to the environment, eroding the ground and disrupting the natural flow of the park. Sometimes, these shortcuts lead to dead ends or rugged terrain that's hard to circumnavigate.

The situation is similar in the digital world. There are plenty of shortcuts to information—viral social media posts, sensational headlines, clickbait articles—but not all lead to the right destination. You risk becoming misinformed, confused, or even in danger when you rely on shortcuts instead of carefully following reliable sources.

Similar to how some shortcut trails in the park might lead to muddy patches or blocked paths, online shortcuts often take you to biased, incomplete, or outright false information. Relying on such information can lead to making wrong decisions, spreading misinformation, or even falling victim to scams or cyberbullying.

Shasha and I often follow specific trails when walking through the nature reserve. Some lead us safely to beautiful sights, while others are overgrown or misleading. Similarly, in the digital world, it's essential to identify reliable sources of information and avoid misleading ones. We have already shared examples of reliable and unreliable sources in chapter 4. The main point is, before believing something, ask: Who wrote this? Where did they get their information? Can I find the same facts from other trusted sources?

Avoiding Misinformation and Fake News

Imagine walking in the park and seeing a sign that says, "Beware of Wolves!" That would be strange, right? There are no wolves in our nature reserve! But if someone didn't think critically, they might panic. Fake news works similarly—it preys on emotions and spreads quickly. So, how do you stay on the right path when maneuvering in the vast online world? Here are a few strategies:

1. *Check the Source*: Just as we trust official park signs over handwritten notes taped to a tree, rely on well-known, credible sources instead of random blogs or social media posts.

2. *Cross-check information*: If something seems surprising or extreme, don't take it at face value. Look up multiple sources to see if they all report the same thing. Can you find the exact information elsewhere?

3. *Be Wary of Clickbait*: If a headline sounds too dramatic or shocking, it might be designed to get clicks rather than tell the whole truth. Read beyond the headline before forming an opinion. Watch out for emotional tricks; if something is designed to make you angry or scared, double-check before believing it.

4. *Pause Before Sharing*: In the park, we didn't immediately believe that feeding birds was terrible—we read the sign, thought about it, and learned more. Similarly, before sharing something online, please take a moment to verify it. Misinformation spreads when people pass it along without checking facts. By taking the time to verify information, you're being responsible and considerate of others.

5. *Look for Context*: Some images or videos online are edited or taken out of context to mislead viewers. A single clip can tell one story, but the whole video might reveal something completely different. Always dig deeper. This thorough approach will help you avoid falling for misleading content and make you a skilled online navigator.

Staying Safe Online

The internet is like a vast, open park—full of exciting discoveries, new paths to explore, and opportunities to connect with others. But just as there are clear signs in a park warning you to stay on designated trails or avoid feeding the birds, there are also important rules to follow online to keep yourself safe.

By using critical thinking, you can protect yourself from misleading information, online scams, and even people who may not have good intentions. Like staying on safe trails in the park, we must be mindful of online dangers. Here are some key rules to follow:

1. *Protect your personal information* - Never share personal details like your full name, home address, phone number, or school location with strangers online. Scammers and cyberbullies often look for this information.

2. *Be cautious with social media* - What you post online can be seen by more people than you think. Ask yourself: Would it be okay if my parents or future boss saw this? Could this hurt someone's feelings or damage my reputation? Am I sharing something private that could be misused? Think before posting, commenting, or sending private messages.

3. *Spot online scams* - If something sounds too good to be true, it probably is! Be wary of messages or emails asking for money, offering prizes, or saying you've won something you never entered. Is the message pressuring me to act quickly? (Scammers love to create urgency.) Never click suspicious links.

4. *Be aware of cyberbullying* - If someone is being rude, threatening, or making you feel uncomfortable online, don't engage. Block the person and report the behavior. Always tell a trusted adult if you feel unsafe.

5. *Recognize online peer pressure* – In real life, friends might encourage you to take risks, like climbing a shaky fence in the park. Online, peer pressure can be just as strong—daring you to participate in viral challenges, spread rumors, or share risky content. Before giving in, think critically:

- Am I doing this because I want to, or because I feel pressured?

- What are the possible consequences?

- Could I regret this later?

6. *Be Aware of Online Strangers* – If someone approached you in the park and asked for personal details, you'd probably be cautious. The same rule applies online. Not everyone is who they claim to be. Keep these in mind:

- Never share your home address, phone number, or school name publicly.

- Be skeptical of new online "friends" who ask for personal information too soon.

- If something feels off, trust your instincts and talk to a trusted adult.

The Digital Footprint: Leaving the Right Mark

Every step you take in a park leaves an imprint, whether it's a deep mark in soft soil or a faint trace on a gravel path. Over time, those footprints may fade, but for a while, they tell a story—where you've been, how fast you were moving, and even the choices you made along the way. The same is true for your online presence. Everything you do on the internet—every post, comment, like, and share—creates a "digital footprint," a lasting record of your activity.

Unlike footprints in the park that eventually wash away with the rain, your digital footprint can stick around indefinitely. Future schools, employers, and even potential friends may look at your past online behavior to get a sense of who you are. A strong, positive digital footprint can open doors and create opportunities, while a careless one can have lasting consequences. What kind of trail are you leaving? Does it reflect the person you want to be?

Be intentional about your digital presence. Before you post consider, will this comment, photo, or video represent you well years from now? Will it help or harm your reputation? Every step you take online leaves a mark. Make sure yours is one you'll be proud of.

Here's how to maintain a positive digital footprint:

- Think before you post – once something is online, it's hard to erase.

- Be kind – treat others online as you would in real life.

- Keep accounts private and only accept requests from people you know.

Applying Critical Thinking in the Digital World

Next time you're online, remember these questions:

- What is the source of this information?

- Does it sound logical, or is it designed to provoke emotions?

- Can I verify this information on other reliable websites?

- Does this seem too good (or too bad) to be true?

- Who benefits from me believing this?

- Would I say or do this in real life?

As the park's designated walkways guide us safely through nature, trustworthy sources help us navigate the internet wisely. But it's up to us to follow them. If we ignore the correct paths and take shortcuts, we risk getting lost in misinformation. By thinking critically—asking questions, checking sources, and staying curious—we can ensure that we make informed decisions both online and in real life.

The internet is a great place to learn, connect, and express yourself, but just like exploring the park, it's important to stay on safe paths. By using critical thinking, you can explore the digital world wisely, making choices that protect you now and in the future.

By staying aware, you'll always find the right track—online and in everyday life. So next time you're online, ask yourself: *Am I following the park signs or wandering down a shortcut trail?* The choice, as always, is yours.

Key Takeaways from Chapter 6

1. **Information Changes Over Time** – Just like the park changed its rules about feeding birds, online information evolves with new research and updates. It's important to stay adaptable and verify facts regularly.

2. **Trust the Right Signs** – Not all information is reliable. Before believing or acting on something online, check the source. Is it credible? Who created it? What is their motive? Can I verify it from other trusted sources? Reliable sources are like official park signs—they guide you safely. In this way you'll avoid misinformation and make smarter decisions online and in life.

3. **Beware of Shortcuts** – Viral posts, clickbait headlines, and sensational articles may seem like quick ways to get information, but they can lead to misinformation. Like shortcut trails in the park, they might seem convenient but often cause more harm than good.

4. **Avoid Misinformation and Fake News** – Just because something is popular or shocking doesn't mean it's true. Always cross-check facts, look for multiple trusted sources, and be wary of emotional manipulation in online content.

5. **Stay Safe Online** – Protect personal information, be cautious on social media, watch out for scams, recognize cyberbullying, and avoid online peer pressure. Treat online interactions like real-life encounters—be mindful of who you trust and engage with.

6. **Your Digital Footprint Matters** – Everything you post online leaves a lasting trace. Future schools, employers, and friends may see your past actions, so think carefully before sharing content. Keep your digital presence positive and respectful.

7. **Balance Online and Offline Learning** – While digital resources offer a wealth of knowledge, real-world experiences provide valuable lessons too. Just like exploring the park teaches you things a screen never could, engaging with people, books, and hands-on activities helps you develop deeper understanding and critical thinking skills.

Exercises

1. **Read the Signs (Spotting Online Misinformation)**

    - Look at the following online headlines. Which ones seem trustworthy? Which ones might be misleading?

    - What "warning signs" (like exaggerated claims, lack of sources, or emotional language) can help you tell the *difference?*

Headlines to evaluate:

- "Scientists say chocolate is the secret to living 150 years!"
- "Local news: Heavy rain expected tomorrow—bring an umbrella!"
- "Click here to see shocking celebrity secrets—#3 will blow your mind!"
- "NASA confirms: Aliens have been living on Earth for decades."

Think About It: What makes some of these headlines more reliable than others?

2. **Shortcuts vs. Safe Paths (Evaluating Sources)**

Below are three different sources about the same topic. Which would you trust the most? Why?

- A TikTok video with no sources but a confident speaker.
- A Wikipedia article with multiple references.
- A government health website explaining the topic in detail.

Think About It: How do you decide which "trail" (source) to take when looking for information online?

3. **Fact-Checking Patrol (Tracing Online Information)**

Pick a viral news story or social media post. Try to find out who originally posted it, is it backed by real experts or official sources, and has it been fact-checked?

Think About It: How often do you check where online info comes from before believing or sharing it?

4. Being Responsible Online

Think of a time you saw false information online.

- *What did people do—did they question, share, or ignore it?*

- *If you had been there, how would you have responded?*

Think About It: What small actions can you take to ensure you're "feeding" the internet with truth, not rumors?

PART III

MAKING DECISIONS & SOLVING PROBLEMS

Sometimes, the best way to speak to someone is to say nothing.

—Andrea Campbell

Chapter Seven

The Grass is Always Greener: Appreciating Different Viewpoints

Have you ever considered someone else's life and thought, "Wow, they have it so much better than me!" Maybe it's the friend who always seems to have the latest phone, the classmate who never seems to struggle with schoolwork, or the person on social media whose life looks perfect. It's easy to assume that others have it better—but is that the whole story?

Shasha and I had a moment like that during one of our walks in the park. We were standing in a vast, open field, surrounded by patches of grass that were a mix of green and brown. It had been a dry season, and most of the field looked parched. But in the distance, something stood out—a section of grass that seemed unbelievably lush and vibrant, like a perfect green carpet in the middle of the duller landscape. It didn't make sense. Why was that single spot so much greener than the rest?

Curious, we decided to check it out. As we got closer, the answer became clear—a small brook ran through that area, consistently nourishing the grass. What seemed magical from afar had a very real, practical explanation. It wasn't luck or some secret formula—it was water. The grass wasn't greener by accident; it had the right conditions to thrive. That tiny moment opened my eyes to a significant truth: what we see from a distance is often misleading.

Understanding Faulty Reasoning

Faulty reasoning is like a weed in a garden. If left unchecked, it can take root, spread, and crowd out clear, healthy thinking. Stopping it early, "nipping it in the bud" is one of the most important skills in critical thinking. This chapter explores how to identify faulty reasoning, recognize when it's starting to grow, and develop strategies to stop it before it causes harm.

Faulty reasoning occurs when the process of drawing conclusions is flawed. It might seem harmless at first—a minor assumption here, a hasty conclusion there—but these errors can quickly multiply, leading to misunderstandings, poor decisions, and even conflict. For example, imagine you see a swan lazily floating away from the other birds on the lake.

You might think swans must be antisocial, but they could be looking for food or protecting their young. Jumping to conclusions without sufficient evidence is one of the most common forms of faulty reasoning. We'll explore this later, but other types include:

1. *Jumping to Conclusions*: Concluding without enough evidence. *Example*: Assuming someone is upset with you because they didn't smile when you greeted them. Another example could be assuming a person is wealthy because they

go abroad frequently, without considering other factors like their job or financial situation.

2. *Confirmation Bias*: Only noticing or accepting evidence that supports your existing beliefs. *Example*: Believing pigeons are dirty birds and ignoring evidence of their intelligence or usefulness.

3. *Ad Hominem*: Attacking the person instead of addressing their argument. *Example*: Dismissing someone's opinion about the park's cleanliness by saying, "What do they know? They don't even recycle!"

4. *False Cause (Post Hoc)*: Assuming that because one thing happened after another, the first caused the second. *Example*: "The swan started swimming away right after we arrived. We must have scared it."

5. *Overgeneralization*: Making broad claims based on limited evidence. *Example*: Seeing one duck aggressively chase another and concluding, "All ducks are mean."

Spotting the Warning Signs

Faulty reasoning often begins subtly. Here are some signs to watch for:

- *Emotional Responses*: Are you feeling defensive, angry, or overly confident? Emotions can cloud judgment and lead to hasty conclusions.

- *Simplistic Explanations*: Are you oversimplifying a complex issue? The most straightforward answer isn't always the right one.

- *Lack of Evidence*: Are you basing your conclusion on assumptions rather than facts?

Faulty reasoning doesn't just affect your thinking—it can also impact your relationships and decisions. For example:

- *In Friendships*: Jumping to conclusions about someone's intentions can lead to unnecessary conflicts.

- *In School or Work*: Relying on incomplete information can result in poor performance or missed opportunities.

- *In Everyday Life*: Overgeneralizing or making assumptions can prevent you from seeing the complete picture.

Avoid these pitfalls and make better choices by addressing faulty reasoning early. By challenging our assumptions and faulty reasoning, we can take control of our thinking and make more informed decisions. This empowerment is the key to personal growth and improved relationships.

The Temptation of Assumptions

When we first noticed the vibrant patch of grass, it was easy to assume that it was simply better soil or better sunlight that made it thrive. However, assumptions are often incomplete. Similarly, in daily life, we judge others based on what we see on the surface. Someone who seems to have an "easier" life or more success might have different circumstances or resources, much like the grass that thrived because of the brook's support.

This analogy serves as a powerful reminder that other people's realities are shaped by their unique experiences, just as ours are. Embracing diverse perspectives requires us to step out of the comfort of our assumptions and explore what lies beneath the surface. It's a path of enlightenment and open-mindedness.

We usually don't see the whole picture when we assume someone else has it easier or better than us. Maybe the person who always has new gadgets works hard at a part-time job to afford them. Perhaps the student who gets top grades struggles with anxiety or pressure at home. Maybe the influencer with the "perfect" life carefully edits their photos to hide their struggles. Just like with the grass, there's always more beneath the surface.

When people have access to resources, support, and opportunities, they often flourish in ways that outsiders may not immediately notice. For example:

- A student excelling in school might have access to extra tutoring or a supportive home environment.

- A colleague who always seems confident may have a strong mentor guiding them.

- A friend progressing in their finances might benefit from a robust support system.

Recognizing the role of support systems in other people's successes allows us to appreciate their stories without envy or resentment. Instead of thinking, "They have it easier," we can ask, "What can I learn from their circumstances, and how can I build similar supports for myself?"

Jumping to Conclusions

It's human nature to make quick judgments, but when we jump to conclusions without understanding the whole story, we risk seeing things unfairly. Imagine a friend cancels plans at the last minute. It's easy to assume they don't care, but what if they had a family emergency or felt overwhelmed? When we take the time to dig deeper, just as Shasha and I did with the green grass, we can uncover the real reasons behind things.

One of the most essential skills in critical thinking is perspective-taking—learning to see things from another person's point of view. Instead of jumping to conclusions, we can practice asking questions:

- What might happen in their lives that I don't know about?

- How would I feel if I were in their situation?

- What factors could be influencing what I'm seeing?

When we ask these questions, we become more open-minded, understanding, and less likely to judge unfairly.

Walking in Someone Else's Shoes

To truly understand others, you must walk in their shoes—metaphorically, of course. This requires empathy and a willingness to see things through their eyes.

Imagine someone you know with a very different opinion than yours on a particular topic. Before dismissing that person's viewpoint, ask yourself:

- What experiences might have led them to this perspective?

- What values or beliefs shape their thinking?

- How might their circumstances differ from my own?

In the park, as we moved closer to the green patch, the view transformed. What had seemed like a distant anomaly became clear and understandable when we approached with curiosity. Similarly, seeking to understand others' perspectives can reveal the richness of their experiences and help bridge gaps in understanding.

Lush grass near a stream

The Grass Isn't Always Greener

The saying "The grass is always greener on the other side" often reflects our tendency to idealize others' situations while underestimating our own. However, a closer look sometimes reveals that the "greener" grass comes with its own set of challenges.

Consider a scenario where someone appears to have a perfect life—perhaps they have a great job, a beautiful home, or a happy relationship. While those external markers may seem enviable, their life might also involve stress, sacrifices, or personal struggles you can't see.

By appreciating different viewpoints, we can avoid falling into the trap of comparison and instead focus on gratitude for what we have. We might also discover that other people look at our lives and think *our "grass is greener" than theirs!*

Expanding Your Perspective

Seeing the world from multiple perspectives is not just about understanding others—it's about expanding your thinking. Appreciating different viewpoints helps you grow and become more adaptable in solving problems or making decisions.

For instance, when you collaborate with a group, everyone brings their perspective. Someone may focus on the big picture, while another pays attention to details. Someone else might approach the problem emotionally, while another takes a logical angle. By combining these diverse viewpoints, the group can arrive at a more balanced and effective solution than any individual could achieve alone.

Shasha and I sometimes follow paths others recommend in the park, even if they don't look appealing initially. This experience often opens our eyes to discoveries we might have missed. Similarly, being open to others' perspectives allows you to gain insights and ideas that enrich your life.

Appreciating different viewpoints is a skill that can be developed with practice. Here are a few exercises to strengthen your perspective-taking abilities:

1. *Ask Open-Ended Questions*: When engaging with someone whose perspective differs from yours, ask questions like:

- "What experiences have shaped your opinion?"
- "How do you see this situation?"
- "What values are most important to you in this decision?"

Listening actively and without judgment fosters a more profound understanding.

2. *Ask "Why?" Five times*: For any conclusion you reach, ask "Why?" five times to dig deeper into your reasoning.

3. *Play Devil's Advocate* - Challenge yourself to argue the opposite side of a vigorously debated issue. This forces you

to see the strengths and weaknesses of both sides and helps you empathize with those who hold opposing views.

4. *Expand Your Circles* - Spend time with people with different backgrounds, cultures, or life experiences. Exposure to diversity broadens your worldview and helps you appreciate perspectives you might not encounter in your usual environment.

5. *Reflect on Your Biases* - We all have biases that influence how we interpret information. Reflect on your assumptions and consider how they might limit your ability to see other viewpoints fairly.

6. *Seek Feedback* - Share your conclusions with someone else and ask for their input. Are there gaps or biases you didn't notice?

The Bigger Picture

As Shasha and I explored the lush patch of grass, we realized that its beauty wasn't simply a matter of chance—it was the result of specific conditions. In the same way, people's circumstances, support systems, and experiences shape their perspectives and outcomes.

When you take the time to appreciate different viewpoints, you gain a richer understanding of the world. You become more empathetic, adaptable, and open to new ideas. And just like finding the brook that nourished the grass, you discover that there's often more to the story than meets the eye.

So, the next time you encounter someone with a perspective that challenges your own, take a step closer. Explore their "field." You might find that their viewpoint holds lessons, insights, or inspiration to help you grow. The next time you think, "They have it so much better than me," take a step back. Ask yourself if you're seeing the whole picture. Like the patch of green grass in the park, the answer might surprise you.

The grass isn't greener because it's better—it's greener because of what nourishes it. When we understand and appreciate that nourishment, we gain more respect for the diversity of perspectives that make our world so vibrant.

Instead of feeling discouraged by what others have, focus on what you can do to create the right conditions for your growth. Maybe that means finding the right "water source"—learning new skills, asking for help, or changing your thoughts about challenges.

Success isn't just a matter of luck; it's about discovering what nourishes you and fuels your growth. Just as deep roots sustain the tallest trees, the right mindset and habits will help you thrive.

By learning to see beyond surface appearances and question what lies beneath, we sharpen our thinking, deepen our understanding, and become more impactful in our lives. And that's a skill worth cultivating—just like the resilient grass that flourishes by the brook, bending with the wind yet standing strong.

Key Takeaways from Chapter 7

1. **Things Aren't Always as They Seem:** We often assume others have it better than us, but like the patch of green grass in the park, success is usually a result of unseen factors—support, effort, or resources.

2. **Faulty Reasoning Can Lead to Poor Conclusions:** Common thinking errors like jumping to conclusions, confirmation bias, and overgeneralization can distort reality and lead to misunderstandings or unfair judgments.

3. **The Role of Support Systems:** Just as the grass thrived due to the brook, people succeed because of hidden support—mentors, education, family, or opportunities. Recognizing this helps us learn rather than envy.

4. **The Danger of Assumptions:** Assuming someone has an "easy" life without knowing their struggles can be misleading. Understanding the full picture fosters empathy and open-mindedness.

5. **Expanding Perspectives Improves Critical Thinking:** Actively challenging our own beliefs, asking "why" multiple times, and considering opposing views help develop a more balanced and thoughtful approach to life.

6. **Avoiding Comparison and Focusing on Growth:** Instead of envying others, we should identify what resources, habits, or strategies we can adopt to create our own success.

7. **The Power of Perspective-Taking:** Walking in someone else's shoes—seeing life from their viewpoint—allows us to be more understanding, adaptable, and insightful in our interactions and decision-making.

REFLECTION EXERCISE

1. Think about a time when you assumed something about a person or situation but later realized you were wrong.

2. What did you learn from that experience?

3. How can you practice looking beyond first impressions in the future?

Chapter Eight

Hidden Thorns: Spotting Common Thinking Traps

As we strolled along the trail, we came upon a stunning rose garden. However, we kept our distance because, while the flowers are lovely, visible and hidden thorns will scratch and cause injuries. Our thinking has "thorns" too—common traps that can snag our reasoning and lead us to incorrect conclusions. Recognizing and avoiding these traps is crucial for developing strong critical thinking skills. It's the first step in taking control of our decisions!

The Most Common Thinking Thorns

1. *The Bandwagon Thorn* - Believing something just because "everyone else" does. *For example*: "All my friends are downloading this app, so it must be good!" How to avoid it: Ask yourself -

- Would I want this if others weren't doing it?

- Does popularity always equal quality?

- What do I think about this?

- Do I need this app?

- What will I benefit from the app, and what will I miss if I don't download it?

2. *The Emotional Cloud Thorn* - Letting feelings overpower logical thinking. *For example*: "I'm so angry at my friend that I won't listen to their side of the story." How to avoid it:

- Take a breath and wait before reacting

- Ask: How and what would I think about this if I wasn't emotional?

- Write down your thoughts to see them more clearly

3. *The Quick Jump Thorn* - Making assumptions without enough evidence. *For example*: "She didn't like my post, so she must be mad at me." How to avoid it:

- List other possible explanations

- Look for actual evidence

- Ask questions before concluding

4. *The Either/Or Thorn* - Thinking there are only two options when there might be more. *For example*: "Either I get perfect grades, or I'm a failure." How to avoid it:

- Look for middle ground

- Brainstorm more options

HIDDEN THORNS: SPOTTING COMMON THINKING TRAPS

- Question extreme thinking

5. *The Memory Trick Thorn* - Remember only what supports your beliefs. *For example*: "Social media is always right because I remember the times it was correct." How to avoid it:

- Look for examples that don't fit your belief
- Keep track of both hits and misses
- Ask others for their experiences

Your Thorn-Spotting Tools

1. The STOP Method – **i)S**top what you're doing, **ii)T**hink about your thinking, **iii) O**bserve any thinking traps, **i) P**roceed with better thinking

2. The Questions Shield

Protect yourself from thinking traps by asking:

- What evidence do I have?
- What am I assuming?
- How do my emotions affect this?
- What would others think about this?
- Are there other possibilities?

3. The Reality Check List

When making a decision, check for:

- Am I following the crowd without thinking?
- Are my emotions too strong right now?

- Am I jumping to conclusions?

- Am I seeing all options?

- Am I only seeing what I want to see?

Beautiful flowering plant but prickly to the touch

Don't Beat Around the Bush

Imagine walking through a dense patch of the nature reserve, where the trees grow close together, and bushes line the path. If you're searching for something specific, like a bird nesting in a shrub, beating around the bush won't help. You need to look carefully, directly, and with purpose. The same is true for critical thinking: when faced with a question or challenge, you'll get the best results by being direct and thoughtful rather than vague or hesitant.

This chapter explores the art of asking direct, thoughtful questions. Questions are the tools that help you dig beneath the surface, uncover hidden truths, and deepen your understanding. Learning to ask the appropriate questions at the right time can clarify your thinking, find new ideas, and most importantly, strengthen your relationships by fostering deeper connections and engagement.

Being direct doesn't mean being blunt or insensitive. It means being honest and intentional about what you want to know. Direct questions build trust and respect, showing that you value clarity and aren't afraid to engage with meaningful topics.

For instance, when Shasha and I explore the nature reserve, she often asks direct, thoughtful questions like, "Why do the ducks come out of the water?" or "Why are the swans so much bigger than the other birds?" These questions spark conversation and deepen her understanding of the world around her, showing the power of direct, thoughtful questions in learning and exploration.

The Problem with Beating Around the Bush

When we "beat around the bush," we avoid addressing the main issue. This could be because we're afraid of offending someone, unsure what to ask, or hesitant to face the truth. While this approach might feel safer in the short term, it often leads to confusion, misunderstandings, and missed opportunities.

For example, imagine you're on a team working on a school project, and something isn't going well. Instead of saying, "Why aren't we meeting our deadlines?" you ask, "How's everyone feeling about the project?" While the second question might be easier to ask, it doesn't address the real problem, leaving everyone unsure about how to move forward.

Learning to ask direct questions is not just about the questions themselves, but about the qualities it requires. It demands courage, clarity, and a willingness to engage with the issue at hand. It's a skill that, when mastered, can lead to deeper understanding and more effective problem-solving.

Why Asking Questions Matters

Asking questions is the gateway to learning. It's how we make sense of the world, challenge assumptions, and seek new perspectives. But not all questions are created equal. Some questions lead to deeper understanding, while others keep you circling the edges of a problem.

Direct questions are like a well-aimed arrow—they cut through confusion and get to the heart of the matter. For example, if you see a bird behaving oddly, asking, "Why is that bird doing that?" is far more productive than vaguely wondering about it. Thoughtful questions, on the other hand, consider context and purpose. They are intentional, showing that you care about understanding the issue or person in front of you.

The Components of a Good Question

Good questions share a few key characteristics. Here's how to craft questions that lead to deeper understanding:

1. *Be Clear and Specific* -Vague questions lead to ambiguous answers. A straightforward, specific question gives others a better sense of your question. *Example:* Instead of asking, "Can you tell me about this bird?" try, "What type of bird is that and why does it have such colorful feathers?"

2. *Be Open-Ended* - Closed questions (those that can be answered with a simple "yes" or "no") have their place, but open-ended questions encourage exploration and dialogue.

Example: Instead of asking "Do you like the nature reserve?" try, "What do you enjoy most about the nature reserve, and why?"

3. *Consider the Context* - A thoughtful question considers the situation, the people involved, and the desired outcome. *Example*: If someone seems upset, asking, "What's bothering you?" is better than diving into unrelated topics.

4. *Be Curious* - Let genuine curiosity guide your questions. When you're genuinely interested in the answer, it shows—and people are likelier to engage with you.

Practical Tips for Asking Better Questions

If you're unsure where to start, here are some tips to help you develop the habit of asking good questions:

1. *Listen First* - Good questions often come from careful listening. Respond to what's being said, and let your curiosity guide your response.

2. *Don't Be Afraid to Pause* - Taking a moment to think before you ask a question shows that you're being intentional.

3. *Practice Asking "Why" and "How"* - These simple words can open up a world of understanding.

4. *Be Respectful* - Frame your questions to show you care about the other person's thoughts and feelings.

Real-Life Applications

Here's how avoiding thinking traps helps in everyday situations:

1. Social Media

- Before sharing posts, check for thinking traps

- Look for evidence behind viral claims
- Consider multiple viewpoints

2. Friendships

    - Avoid jumping to conclusions about others' actions
    - Look for alternative explanations
    - Keep emotions in check during conflicts

3. School

    - Question common assumptions about subjects or assignments
    - Look beyond either/or thinking in problem-solving
    - Check emotional reactions to grades or feedback

Everyone falls into thinking traps sometimes. The key is learning to spot them and finding better ways to think. Keep practicing, and you'll get better at avoiding these thorns in your thinking garden.

The quality of your questions shapes the quality of your thinking. Don't beat around the bush—be direct, be thoughtful, and let your curiosity lead the way. With practice, you'll find that asking the right questions opens doors to understanding, growth, and connection. In the next chapter, we'll explore "An Olive Branch" which explains how to approach conflicts wisely. The skills you've learned here will help you recognize when thinking traps might distort your decisions.

Key Takeaways from Chapter 8

1. **Recognizing Thinking Traps** – Just like hidden thorns in a rose garden, certain thinking patterns—such as jumping to conclusions, emotional reasoning, and following the crowd—can lead to poor decisions. Learning to spot and avoid these "thorns" strengthens critical thinking.

2. **The STOP Method for Better Thinking** – Before making a decision, pause and analyze your thought process: **S**top what you're doing; **T**hink about your thinking; **O**bserve any thinking traps; **P**roceed with better reasoning.

3. **Asking the Right Questions** – Avoiding thinking traps starts with asking smart, direct, and thoughtful questions. Instead of being vague or hesitant, approach problems with curiosity and precision to uncover deeper truths.

4. **Emotions Can Cloud Judgment** – Feelings like anger or excitement can distort logical thinking. Taking a moment to reflect and asking, "How would I think about this if I wasn't emotional?" helps in making clearer decisions.

5. **The Power of Open-Mindedness** – Thinking traps often limit perspectives. By considering multiple viewpoints, questioning extreme thinking, and looking beyond assumptions, we expand our understanding of any situation.

6. **Real-Life Applications of Critical Thinking** – Whether in social media, friendships, or school, avoiding thinking traps helps in making informed choices, resolving conflicts, and improving

problem-solving skills.

7. **Be Direct, Not Blunt** – Being clear and intentional in asking questions leads to better understanding and connection with others. Avoiding indirect or vague questioning prevents confusion and fosters meaningful conversations.

Practice Exercises

1. Thorn Detector – *For one day, keep track of thinking traps you notice: in your thinking, in social media posts, in conversations with friends, in advertisements and in your reactions to events.*

2. Thought Detective – *Pick a recent decision you made and investigate: what thinking traps might have influenced you, how you could have thought about it differently, and what you would do differently next time.*

3. Group Challenge – *With friends or family, play "Spot the Thinking Trap." Share examples of thinking traps you've fallen into, help each other find better ways to think and practice using the Questions Shield together.*

Reflection Questions

1. Which thinking trap do you fall into most often?
2. What's one situation where spotting a thinking trap could help you?
3. How could you help a friend avoid one of these thinking traps?

CHAPTER NINE

An Olive Branch: Approaching Conflicts Wisely

CONFLICT IS AN INEVITABLE PART of life. Whether it's a disagreement with a classmate over a social media issue, a misunderstanding with a friend over a social matter, or a family argument about household responsibilities, we all encounter situations where differing perspectives clash. How we approach these moments can make the difference between escalation and resolution.

Approaching Conflicts Wisely

During one of our visits to the nature reserve, we witnessed a striking lesson in conflict management. As we were walking in the open area, we came across a large bird pecking aggressively at a smaller bird of a different species, attempting to assert dominance. Just as it seemed the smaller bird might be harmed, another bird, perhaps its parent, swooped in. But instead of attacking the aggressor, this third bird calmly and decisively removed the smaller bird from harm's way. The larger bird, now ignored, eventually lost interest and flew off.

This simple yet profound act is a powerful illustration of the power of de-escalation and protection, over confrontation. In this chapter, we explore how we can take a cue from nature and approach conflicts with wisdom, calmness, and intention.

The Instinct to Fight or Flee

Our instincts often kick in in conflicts: we fight back or flee. These responses are part of our survival mechanisms but are not always the most effective strategies for resolving interpersonal disagreements.

The bird's behavior demonstrated a third approach—neither fight nor flight, but thoughtful intervention. It prioritized safety over retaliation and resolution over revenge. This approach, symbolized by offering an "olive branch" (a symbol of peace and reconciliation), can be a powerful way to manage conflict in our own lives.

Understanding the Root Cause

Before responding to any conflict, it's important to understand its root cause. Conflicts often arise from:

- *Misunderstandings*: Different communication styles or incomplete information can lead to unnecessary disagreements.

- *Clashing Values*: Conflicts can occur when people have deeply held beliefs or priorities that are at odds.

- *Unmet Needs*: When individuals feel ignored, undervalued, or unsupported, tensions can escalate.

AN OLIVE BRANCH: APPROACHING CONFLICTS WISELY

By taking the time to identify what's really at the heart of a conflict, you can respond more effectively and avoid escalating the situation further. This understanding can bring a sense of relief, as it empowers you to manage conflicts with clarity and insight. For example, had the larger bird's aggression been retaliated with equal force, the problem might have spiraled into chaos. Instead, the third bird's calm actions shifted the dynamic entirely.

Peculiar-shaped tree seeming to offer an olive branch

De-escalation: A Critical Skill

De-escalation involves reducing the intensity of a conflict rather than feeding into it. The key to this skill lies in controlling your emotions and choosing actions that diffuse tension rather than inflame it. This sense of control can be empowering, as it allows you to steer the conflict towards a more constructive resolution.

Here are steps to de-escalate conflicts:

1. *Pause and Breathe*: Take a moment to center yourself. Reacting impulsively often leads to regret.

2. *Listen Actively*: Hear the other person's perspective without interrupting or judging. Sometimes, simply feeling heard can calm someone down.

3. *Acknowledge Feelings*: Validate the emotions involved, even if you disagree with the other person's stance. For example, saying, "I understand this is frustrating for you," can build a bridge.

4. *Stay Neutral*: Avoid accusatory language and focus on the issue, not the person. Replace "You always..." with "I feel..." statements to keep the conversation constructive.

In the park, the bird didn't waste energy confronting the bully. Instead, it focused on protecting the vulnerable smaller bird and neutralizing the danger. Similarly, you can choose to prioritize resolution over retaliation.

Perspective and Emotional Intelligence

Perspective-taking is a key element in emotional intelligence. It allows us to empathize with others and build meaningful connections. For instance, stepping back to consider the other person's viewpoint during a heated argument can diffuse tension and lead to a more productive conversation.

Imagine a friend is upset because you canceled plans. From your perspective, you had a legitimate reason, perhaps you were overwhelmed with work. But from their perspective, your absence might feel like neglect or indifference. Understanding their feelings doesn't mean you were wrong, but it helps you address the situation with empathy and clarity.

The Power of Empathy

One of the most effective ways to resolve conflicts is to step into the other person's shoes and view the situation from their perspective. Empathy helps us understand what the other person is saying and why they feel the way they do.

Imagine you're in a disagreement with a friend. Instead of thinking, *Why are they being so unreasonable?* Ask yourself:

- What might they be experiencing that's contributing to this conflict?
- How might their values or priorities differ from mine in this situation?
- What can I do to show them I value our relationship, even if we don't see eye to eye?

In our observation of the birds discussed earlier, the protective bird showed empathy by recognizing the smaller bird's vulnerability. Its actions weren't about "winning" or "proving who is stronger" but ensuring safety and harmony. It is often better to walk away, even if you are limping, than to stand firm in the wrong place.

Choosing Your Battles

Not every conflict is worth engaging in. Some disagreements are best resolved by stepping away or letting go, primarily when rooted in misunderstandings or trivial issues.

A few questions to help decide whether a conflict is worth addressing:

- Does this conflict affect my values or priorities?
- Is there potential for growth or understanding by addressing it?
- Will resolving this conflict strengthen the relationship or situation?

The parent bird understood this intuitively. It chose not to retaliate against the bully bird because engaging in a fight would have only escalated the conflict. Instead, it focused on protecting the smaller bird and maintaining peace.

Offering an Olive Branch

Extending an olive branch means taking the first step toward reconciliation, even when it feels difficult. It requires humility, courage, and a genuine desire for resolution. When you offer an olive branch, you can feel a sense of accomplishment, knowing that you've taken a proactive step toward resolving the conflict.

Here's how you can offer an olive branch in conflicts:

1. *Apologize When Necessary*: Owning up to your part in the conflict shows maturity and accountability.

2. *Seek Common Ground*: Focus on shared goals or values to overcome disagreements.

3. *Propose Solutions*: Offer practical ways to resolve the issue and move forward.

4. *Practice Forgiveness*: Letting go of grudges helps restore relationships and allows you to focus on the future rather than the past.

In the park, the olive branch was metaphorical. The third bird effectively resolved the conflict by ignoring the aggressor and protecting the smaller bird. Its actions remind us that sometimes, peace is achieved not through confrontation but through thoughtful, non-aggressive solutions.

The Ripple Effect of Wise Conflict Resolution

How you handle conflicts can have a lasting impact on your relationships and environment. When you choose to de-escalate, empathize, and offer an olive branch, you set a positive example for others.

Imagine a school where classmates handle disagreements with respect, patience, and an open mind. Instead of drama and division, there's a vibe of trust, teamwork, and shared goals. When people communicate and work through conflicts wisely, friendships deepen, group projects become more manageable, and everyone feels more supported. The same is true for family and close friends; learning to handle conflicts with understanding and empathy makes relationships stronger and more meaningful.

The bird's choice to prioritize protection over retaliation rippled through the situation, leading to peace. In your own life, each choice you make in resolving conflicts contributes to a broader ripple effect of harmony and understanding.

A Lesson from the Birds

As we watched the bird's graceful handling of conflict, it struck me how much we could learn from nature. The situation wasn't about dominance or winning but protecting what mattered and preserving peace.

Approaching conflicts wisely doesn't mean avoiding them altogether. It means facing them with a clear head, an open heart, and a focus on resolution. By offering an olive branch instead of raising a fist, you can turn potential battles into opportunities for growth and connection.

The next time you find yourself in a conflict, think of the protective bird. Ask yourself:

- What outcome do I truly want?
- How can I resolve this without escalating it?
- What steps can I take to protect what matters most?

Resilient Thinking

Resilient thinking is like a tree standing firm in the face of a storm. It doesn't mean avoiding problems or never feeling shaken; it means bending with the wind rather than breaking, finding a way forward no matter the challenge. It's the ability to stay flexible, focused, and determined when problems emerge.

Nature is the perfect teacher of resilience. The trees in the park sway in the wind, but their deep roots keep them firmly grounded. Birds don't panic when the seasons change; they adjust, migrate, and find new ways to thrive. Even the smallest blades of grass push through cracks in the pavement, refusing to be held back. This resilience, the ability to adapt, recover, and keep growing, is nature's quiet superpower. And just like nature, your mind can develop the same strength.

On one of our visits, after a storm, we saw broken branches scattered across the ground, muddy puddles everywhere, and the air carried a slight stench. However, despite the disruption, life continued. The trees still stood, their roots gripping the soil. Birds emerged from shelter, calling to one another as if making plans. Even the flowers, battered by the wind, lifted their heads toward the sun. The storm had passed, and the park was already recovering.

This is the power of resilience, not just in nature but in life. You will face setbacks. You will encounter moments that shake you. But like the trees, the birds, and the smallest sprout breaking through the earth, you can endure and grow stronger. Resilient thinking means seeing obstacles not as roadblocks but as stepping stones, learning from failures instead of fearing them, and believing that no matter how strong the storm, you can withstand it and thrive again.

From Resilient Thinking to Resilient Living

Resilience isn't just a mindset, it's a way of life. When you approach life with resilience, you don't just survive; you thrive. Challenges become stepping stones, and setbacks become setups for comebacks.

As we continued our walk through the park, we noticed how quickly the birds had returned after the storm. They resumed their activities as if nothing had happened, their resilience a quiet yet powerful reminder of life's ability to recover and flourish.

Let nature be your guide as you cultivate your resilience. Stand firm, adapt when necessary, and let your strength shine through. With each step forward, you're becoming a force of nature, unstoppable, unshakable, and ready for anything.

Practice Makes Peace

Conflict is part of life but doesn't have to be destructive. By learning to approach disagreements with wisdom, calmness, and empathy, you can transform challenges into opportunities for growth and connection.

As we left the park that day, I reflected on how much that simple encounter between the birds taught me. In a world where aggression often seems like the first response, choosing to offer an olive branch instead can be a powerful act of courage and wisdom.

Approaching conflicts wisely is not about avoiding difficult conversations—it's about handling them with care, clarity, and a focus on resolution. Whether you're managing a disagreement at home, school, or work, remember that the choice to extend understanding and offer peace is always within your power.

In the end, conflicts don't have to divide us. With the right mindset and skills, they can bring us closer together, deepening our understanding of one another and creating a ripple effect of harmony in our relationships and communities. Each conflict is an opportunity to grow. By approaching it with intention and care, you resolve the immediate issue and strengthen your ability to handle future challenges.

The next chapter: "The Ripple Effect," will help you understand cause and effect, but for now, remember that sometimes, the greatest strength lies not in fighting but in knowing when to step back, extend understanding, and offer peace.

Key Takeaways from Chapter 9

1. **Conflict is Inevitable, but Response is a Choice** - Disagreements are a natural part of life, but how we handle them determines whether they escalate or lead to resolution.

2. **There's More Than Just Fight or Flight** – Instead of reacting with aggression or avoidance, a third option, thoughtful intervention, can lead to better outcomes.

3. **Understanding the Root Cause Leads to Better Solutions** – Many conflicts stem from misunderstandings, clashing values, or unmet needs. Identifying these helps in addressing the real issue rather than just the surface disagreement.

4. **De-escalation is a Powerful Conflict-Resolution Skill** – Pausing, listening actively, and responding calmly can prevent conflicts from spiraling out of control.

5. **Empathy Builds Bridges, Not Walls** – Viewing situations from another person's perspective can reduce tension and foster stronger relationships.

6. **Not Every Battle is Worth Fighting** – Learning to choose which conflicts to engage in and which to let go can help conserve energy and maintain peace.

7. **Offering an Olive Branch Shows Strength, Not Weakness** – Taking the first step toward reconciliation requires courage, maturity, and emotional intelligence, ultimately leading to stronger connections and positive ripple effects.

Exercises

Like any skill, resolving conflicts wisely takes practice. Each disagreement presents an opportunity to refine your ability to navigate challenging situations with grace. Here are some exercises you can try to strengthen your conflict-resolution skills:

1. **Role-Playing Scenarios:** Partner with a friend or family member to practice handling hypothetical conflicts. Take turns playing both sides, focusing on de-escalation and empathy.

2. **Journaling Reflections:** After a disagreement, write about what happened. Analyze your actions, the other person's perspective, and what could have been done differently.

3. **Active Listening Exercises:** Practice listening to others without interrupting or formulating your response while they speak. Genuinely understanding someone's viewpoint is key to resolving conflicts effectively.

PART IV

Growth, Adaptability, & Resilience

```
If you can't do it alone,
do it together; and if
you can't go together, go
it alone.
```

—Andrea Campbell

Chapter Ten

The Ripple Effect: Understanding Cause and Effect

This was a sunny afternoon with a light breeze, and we paused by the edge of the lake. The water was still, reflecting the surrounding trees like a mirror. Shasha bent down, picked up a small pebble, and tossed it into the water. The pebble disappeared beneath the surface, but its impact was immediately visible. Ripples radiated outward, growing larger and larger until they reached the far edge of the lake.

Understanding Actions and Consequences

She smiled as she watched the circles expand. Her simple action created an effect that lingered long after the pebble had sunk. It struck me as a perfect metaphor for life: every action we take, no matter how small, sends ripples through our world. This realization equips us to make thoughtful decisions and become responsible, empathetic individuals.

Gentle ripples on the lake

The Anatomy of a Ripple

The ripple effect begins with a single act, like the toss of a pebble. In life, these "pebbles" can be kind words or gestures, careless remarks, thoughtful decisions, or moments of inaction. Our choices impact us and those around us, sometimes in ways we can't immediately see. Understanding this cause-and-effect relationship is key to becoming a critical thinker.

Actions Create Consequences

Consider how the ripples from Shasha's pebble traveled far beyond the initial splash. Our actions, too, can have far-reaching consequences. Immediate consequences are the direct results of an action, like the splash when the pebble hits the water. Secondary consequences emerge over time, like the ripples expanding outward. For instance, a kind word might inspire someone to pay it forward, creating a chain of positivity. Unintended consequences are outcomes we don't anticipate, such as if the pebble had hit and injured a bird rather than falling into the lake.

Recognizing the Ripples in Your Life

Take a moment to think about a recent decision you made. Maybe it was choosing to study for a test instead of going out with friends. That decision might have immediate consequences, like missing out on a fun evening, and long-term benefits, like a better grade or deeper understanding of the material. Reflect on these consequences and how they might have affected you and others in your life.

Similarly, consider how small actions—like smiling at a stranger or helping a classmate—can brighten someone's day and encourage them to do the same for others. These ripples of kindness can spread farther than you imagine.

Building Confidence in Decision-Making

When we reflect on decisions, both big and small, it's clear that confidence plays a crucial role. The more we practice making decisions, the more confidence we build. This doesn't mean that every choice will be easy or that we won't face doubts, but with each decision, we grow in our ability to trust ourselves.

For example, as Shasha and I walked through the dense woods, we realized confidence wasn't about knowing exactly what would happen next but about trusting that we'd handle whatever came our way. Life will present you with challenges and uncertainties, but developing the habit of trusting your judgment will make these moments less intimidating.

Learning from your Decisions

One of the key elements of growing as a decision-maker is learning from each choice we make. There's no such thing as a "perfect" decision, and mistakes are inevitable. What truly matters is how you reflect, adapt, and move forward. Each option, whether it leads to success or a setback, offers valuable lessons that shape your thinking and strengthen your ability to manage future challenges. The more you learn from your experiences, the more confident and capable you become in making wiser, more informed decisions.

After our passage through the dense trail, I reflected on the lessons learned:

1. *Sometimes, the more arduous path brings the most valuable lessons*: We could've taken the easier route, but we chose the one that taught us perseverance, adaptability, and teamwork.

2. *Inaction can be a decision*: Had we stood at the crossroads too long, we would have missed the adventure. Inaction can also carry consequences, often delaying growth or progress.

3. *It's okay to reassess*: Even after deciding, we can reassess. If something feels off or if new information arises, we have the power to change course. This reassurance gives us the freedom to adjust our decisions as needed.

Making decisions isn't about carving your path in stone—it's about staying flexible, open-minded, and willing to grow. Every choice you make is a stepping stone, not a final destination. As you gain new experiences and insights, you can adjust your course, refine your approach, and make better choices. Growth comes from adapting, not from fearing change.

The Power of Decisiveness

Making decisions quickly and decisively is a form of strength in many ways. Hesitating too long or second-guessing yourself constantly can cause stress, confusion, and feeling stuck. By practicing decisiveness, we begin to trust ourselves more, and that confidence, in turn, makes decision-making easier.

Sometimes, quick decisions are necessary, particularly when time is limited. For instance, if you're at a crossroads and need to make a choice quickly, the faster you make the decision, the sooner you can move forward. Even if the decision is imperfect, taking action quickly helps you stay on track and not waste precious time second-guessing.

Overcoming the Fear of Mistakes

Fear of making mistakes is a key obstacle to making confident decisions. No one wants to fail, and the thought of choosing the wrong path can paralyze us with anxiety. However, it's essential to understand that mistakes are an inevitable part of life—and they are often the most effective teachers.

When we faced the fork in the road, I reminded her there was no "wrong" path. Whether we took the dense, challenging trail or the easy, shaded path, we would still experience the beauty of the woods and learn something new along the way. Mistakes are simply opportunities to reassess and adjust our course.

The more comfortable we become with the idea of failure, the easier it is to make decisions without fear. Mistakes don't define us; how we respond to them does.

The Butterfly Effect

The ripple effect is closely related to the concept of the butterfly effect, which suggests that even small actions can lead to significant changes over time. For example, spending an hour daily on a new hobby could lead to mastering a skill, meeting new people, and even opening career opportunities.

The Positive Power of Ripples

Harnessing the ripple effect for good starts with mindfulness. Ask yourself:

- What kind of ripples do I want to create?
- How will my actions affect others?

Here are some positive ripples that you may want to create:

1. *Waves of Kindness* - Kindness is one of the most potent pebbles you can toss into the water. A simple act, like helping someone in need, can inspire a chain reaction of generosity.

2. *Waves that Build Positive Habits* - Small, consistent actions like studying a little daily or practicing gratitude create ripples that lead to long-term success and happiness.

3. *Waves that Advocate for Change* - Standing up for what's right, even in small ways, can inspire others to do the same. Change often starts with one voice, one action, or one idea.

The Danger of Negative Ripples

Just as positive actions create uplifting ripples, negative actions can spread harm. Gossip, unkind words, or reckless decisions can hurt others and damage relationships. Being aware of this helps us make better choices. Here are some examples of actions you can take to avoid the danger of negative ripples:

1. *Avoid Thoughtless Actions* - Pause before speaking or acting. Ask yourself, "What impact could this have?"

2. *Take Responsibility* - If you realize your actions have caused harm, make amends and compensate for them. A sincere apology can help repair the damage.

3. *Learn from Mistakes* - Negative ripples are growth opportunities. Reflect on what went wrong and how you can do better next time.

The Ripple Effect in Critical Thinking

Understanding the ripple effect isn't just about being mindful of your actions—it's about thinking critically about the consequences of your decisions. Before you act, consider:

- *Short-Term Impact:* What will happen immediately?
- *Long-Term Impact: What effect* might this have on me and others?
- *Who will be Affected:* Who will feel the ripples of my actions?

For example, imagine you're deciding to confront a friend about something that upset you. The immediate consequence might be an uncomfortable conversation, but the long-term impact could be a stronger, more honest relationship.

The Role of Intention in the Ripple Effect

The ripples we create are shaped not just by our actions but also by our intentions. Acting purposefully ensures that our ripples are meaningful and aligned with our values.

Set Clear Intentions. Before making a decision, ask yourself:

- What do I hope to achieve?
- How does this align with my values?
- Who might be affected by this?

Evaluate your impact. Regularly reflect on the ripples you've created and consider, are they contributing to the kind of world you want to live in? If not, consider how you can adjust your actions to align more closely with your goals.

One of the most empowering aspects of the ripple effect is realizing that you have control over the type of ripples you create. You don't have to wait for others to act—you can lead by example. Your behavior sets the tone for those around you. Take the initiative, if you see an opportunity to improve a situation, act on it. Stay committed to the process because positive ripples often require persistence and time before you can see results.

Ripples in Relationships

The ripple effect is particularly evident in our interactions with others. A kind word can brighten someone's day, while a careless comment can linger and cause harm. Being mindful of your words and actions in relationships is crucial. Practice empathy: Before responding to someone, please take a moment to consider their perspective. This slight pause can help you communicate more effectively and avoid unnecessary conflict. Acknowledge and appreciate: Expressions of gratitude, no matter how small, can strengthen relationships and encourage positivity. Think of it as tossing pebbles of appreciation into the waters of your connections.

Expanding Ripples: Small Actions, Big Impacts

Sometimes, the most profound changes come from the simplest acts. Think of historical figures whose seemingly small choices created lasting ripples. Rosa Parks' decision to remain seated on a bus sparked a movement. Greta Thunberg's solitary climate strike inspired millions. These are examples of how a single pebble, tossed with courage and conviction, can resonate far and wide.

You don't need to make grand gestures to create meaningful ripples. Everyday actions, like encouraging a friend, sharing knowledge, or practicing empathy, can significantly impact. Over time, these ripples accumulate, creating waves of change in your life and the lives of others.

After Shasha tossed her pebble into the lake, she picked up a larger one. Though she didn't say it, she considered creating a more expansive ripple. When she eventually tossed it into the water, it landed with a splash and a wider ripple. The same is true in life. The size and reach of our ripples depend on the weight of our actions and how we choose to act. Some decisions have minor, localized effects, while others can ripple outward, touching lives far beyond our own.

Lessons from the Lake

As we continued our walk around the lake, I was reminded that life is interconnected, and every action we take matters. When we act with intention and awareness, we can create ripples that uplift ourselves and those around us. Whether through kindness, thoughtful decisions, or positive habits, we can impact the world with our pebbles.

With its ever-expanding ripples, the lake teaches us that change is constant and inevitable. As the water adjusts to the pebbles tossed into it, the world around us responds to our actions. The question is, how will we choose to influence it?

Tossing a pebble is a reminder that every moment is an opportunity to make a difference. The ripples we create define our legacy, whether through small, everyday decisions or larger, life-changing choices. As you move forward, remember that you are constantly tossing pebbles into the water, through your actions, words, and thoughts.

Make each count, and watch as the ripples spread far beyond what you can see. What pebble will you toss into the water today?

Building on the Ripples

Now that we've explored the concept of the ripple effect, it's time to apply this understanding to the next stage. The upcoming chapter, "Park Benches," will cover the power of pause and reflection. Just as ripples can intersect and merge, so too can our lives and actions, creating opportunities for connection and understanding. Let's continue to travel this path together, one thoughtful step at a time.

Key Takeaways from Chapter 10

1. **Every Action Creates a Ripple** – Just like a pebble tossed into a lake, every choice we make sends ripples through our lives and the lives of others. Even small actions, like a kind word or a moment of inaction, can have lasting effects.

2. **Consequences Can Be Immediate, Delayed, or Unexpected** – Actions have direct and indirect outcomes. Some ripples appear instantly (like the splash of the pebble), while others unfold over time (like expanding waves). There are also unintended consequences that we may not anticipate.

3. **Decision-Making Builds Confidence** – Making choices, reflecting on outcomes, and learning from experience strengthen our decision-making skills. Even mistakes serve as valuable lessons, teaching

resilience and adaptability.

4. **Positive Ripples Can Create Lasting Change** – Acts of kindness, positive habits, and standing up for what's right can inspire others, leading to a chain reaction of positive impact. Small, consistent actions accumulate over time, shaping our character and our world.

5. **Negative Ripples Can Spread Harm** – Just as positive ripples uplift, negative actions—like gossip, careless words, or reckless decisions—can create waves of harm. Being mindful of our impact helps us avoid unnecessary conflict and damage.

6. **Intention Shapes the Ripples We Create** – Our actions are most powerful when guided by clear intentions. Being purposeful in what we say and do ensures that our ripples align with our values and contribute to a better world.

7. **We Are Always Tossing Pebbles** – Life is a continuous cycle of action and reaction. Every day, we create ripples through our words, choices, and interactions. By acting with awareness and responsibility, we can ensure that our ripples spread positivity and growth.

EXERCISE

Mapping Your Ripples

1. *Think of a Recent Action:* Write down one decision or action you took this week.

2. *Identify the Ripples:* List the immediate, secondary, and potential long-term consequences.

3. *Evaluate the Impact: Reflect on whether the ripples were positive or negative.*

4. *Plan Future Actions: Consider what you could do differently next time to create more positive ripples.*

Chapter Eleven

Park Benches: The Power of Pause and Reflection

We'd been walking for hours, my phone buzzing with notifications I was trying to ignore. That's when we spotted them – a cluster of wooden park benches encircling a flower garden like a tranquil oasis. One bench in particular, seemed to whisper our names. Without saying a word, we gravitated towards it, the smooth metal slats offering a peaceful respite from the continuous walking.

In that moment, surrounded by the gentle hum of nature, we discovered something profound about the art of thinking. Stopping to rest revealed how rarely we genuinely observe and reflect daily. Just as these benches were strategically placed around the garden to offer moments of rest and fresh perspectives, we, too, need to introduce deliberate pauses in our thinking process.

The Power of the Pause

From our vantage point, we observed it all. Bees lazily flitting between purple and yellow blooms, a butterfly alighting on a nearby bush, its wings a rhythmic dance. In the distance, other visitors strolled along the paths, each lost in their own world. This moment of scrutiny was a revelation, a testament to the power of the pause in sharpening our awareness.

That's when it hit me – all the best decisions I'd made recently had one thing in common: I'd taken time to pause and think them through. Like when I nearly posted an angry comment on John's controversial social media post last week. Instead, I'd put my phone down, take a walk, and send him a private message asking about his perspective. We'd had a great conversation, and I learned things I never knew about his situation. At that time, I was stuck on a work project. Instead of panicking, I'd taken a break, and during dinner, the perfect idea came to me, and the project ended just fine.

"Mommy, let's go!" Shasha nudged me, interrupting my thoughts. As a neurodiverse child, Shasha doesn't talk much but understands enough to know that I was thinking deeply.

"I just realized something, hun. We need to do this more often, but yes, let's go!"

Your park bench isn't about a bench; it can be anywhere. A 'mental park bench' is a metaphor for a moment of pause and reflection, a place where you can sit with your thoughts and observe them without the rush of immediate reactions.

Why Taking a Pause Matters

Think of your mind as a busy nature reserve. Thoughts, like visitors, constantly moving - some rushing, others wandering or playing on the open fields. In the same way that park benches offer visitors a place to rest and observe, mental pauses give your thoughts space to settle and organize themselves.

The Three S's of the Park Bench Principle

1. *Stop*: Learning to pause your thinking process is crucial. This isn't about stopping thoughts altogether (which is impossible) but about stepping back from the rush of immediate reactions.

2. *Sit*: Once you stop, settle into the moment. Finding a comfortable position on a park bench means allowing yourself to be present with your thoughts without immediately trying to solve or change anything.

3. *Survey*: From a park bench, you can observe the whole garden - the pattern of paths, the flow of visitors, and the arrangement of flowers. Similarly, a mental pause—a moment of deliberate reflection and observation—lets you

survey your thoughts, feelings, and the connections between them. This third step of the 'Park Bench Principle' is a crucial part of the process of making more thoughtful decisions.

Let's put these into practice and conduct a 5-minute park bench reflection exercise.

- Find a quiet spot
- Set a timer for 5 minutes
- Focus on observing your thoughts without judgment
- Notice patterns in your thinking
- Write down any insights that emerge

Purposeful Pausing

The practice of purposeful pausing reveals its value in countless everyday situations. When faced with challenges, the initial impulse might be to dive in immediately or, conversely, to procrastinate out of frustration. However, observing the task from a mental park bench often reveals new approaches or helps break down seemingly overwhelming projects into manageable steps. Let's explore how this may look in practice:

In Social Media: When responding to a challenging text or social media post, instead of immediately reacting to provocation, take a "park bench moment" to consider:

- What's the larger context?
- What might be missing from this story?
- How might different perspectives view this?

In School: When feeling overwhelmed by homework or when facing a complex project:

- Pause to break down the task
- Observe what makes it challenging
- Consider different approaches before diving in

In Relationships: During disagreements, when trying to solve complex problems, or in handling feedback or criticism:

- Use the pause to understand your emotions
- Consider the other person's perspective
- Think about the long-term consequences of your response

Here are a few situations when it might be helpful to consider a park bench moment:

- Before hitting 'send' on any angry message
- When we're stuck on a hard homework problem
- After getting into an argument
- Before making any decision involving money
- When trying to figure out if something online is true
- When someone's pressuring you to make a quick choice

The Power of the Pause in Teenage Problem-solving

The modern adolescent brain faces unprecedented information, decisions, and pressures. Social media feeds scroll endlessly, group chats ping continuously, and the demand for instant responses has become the norm. In this rushing stream of data and decisions, pausing and reflecting have become valuable and essential for clear thinking.

Consider how a park bench serves its purpose in a busy park. It doesn't stop the activity around it – people still walk past, birds continue to fly overhead, and the wind still rustles through the trees. Instead, it provides a stable vantage point to observe and understand all these motions. Similarly, taking a moment to pause doesn't mean stopping our thoughts entirely. Instead, it creates a mental space to observe our thinking processes more clearly.

This same principle of purposeful pausing applies to problem-solving and decision-making. Quick judgments often miss crucial details and connections that become apparent only through careful reflection. Whether analyzing a historical event for a school project or evaluating the credibility of an online source, the quality of our thinking improves dramatically when we allow ourselves these moments of contemplation.

The power of the pause extends beyond academic or social scenarios into the realm of personal growth and self-understanding. Regular moments of reflection help us recognize patterns in our thinking, identify our biases, and understand our emotional responses. These insights prove invaluable in developing stronger critical thinking skills and making better decisions.

Reflective pauses reduce stress and anxiety and improve the quality of your decisions and creativity in problem-solving. Taking a moment to pause also boosts your memory and enhances your learning. Like the park benches in our nature reserve, moments of pause and reflection are opportunities. They're not delays or waste of time - they're powerful tools for better thinking and decision-making.

In our age of constant information and immediate responses, pausing and reflecting might be one of the most valuable skills you can develop.

The Value of Reflection in Learning

It's not enough to make decisions or solve problems; we must take the time to reflect on our experiences and learn from them. This is a crucial part of thinking critically and applying it to real life.

After each of our walks, Shasha and I would sit on a bench by the lake and reflect on our experiences. We'd talk about what we learned—whether about the birds we observed, the plants we discovered, or the paths we took. We'd also think about what we could do differently next time. This reflective practice helped us make sense of the process and enhanced our ability to navigate future walks with more insight.

In life, we also need to build in time for reflection. After making decisions or tackling challenges, it's important to pause and think about what worked and what didn't. Did we take the right approach? What could we have done differently? What did we learn from the experience? Reflection helps us refine our thinking and become better at applying critical thinking in the future. By learning from our mistakes and celebrating our successes, we continue to grow.

Lessons from the Garden

The garden around our bench offered a lesson on the value of patient observation. At first glance, we saw only a general impression of colors and movement. But as we sat quietly, details emerged. The bees moved with purpose between specific flowers. Patterns in the garden design became apparent. The interplay of light and shadow revealed new dimensions of the landscape. Our pause had transformed a simple garden into a masterclass in the rewards of patient observation. Sometimes, the best thoughts happen when we stop and observe.

In an age where information moves at the speed of light and decisions are often made with a single click, taking time to reflect might seem outdated. Yet, like the enduring utility of park benches in our increasingly rushed world, purposeful pausing remains a cornerstone of clear thinking and wise decision-making. The challenge lies not in finding time to pause – such moments are always available – but in recognizing their value and purposefully incorporating them into our daily lives.

As the afternoon light softened, our rest on the park bench had become more than a simple break from walking. It had transformed into a lesson in the art of thinking itself. The bench offered a physical place to rest and demonstrated how strategic pauses enhance our ability to observe, understand, and respond to the world.

In a world that's always rushing, sometimes the smartest thing you can do is sit down and observe. Your park bench is waiting. In the realm of social interactions, moments of pause and reflection prove equally valuable. The immediate impulse to respond to provocative messages can lead to regrettable actions. A mental pause creates space to consider alternative perspectives, examine our emotional responses, and craft more thoughtful reactions.

As we progress in our exploration of critical thinking skills, remember that sometimes, the most powerful step we can take is to stop moving altogether momentarily. These chapters examine various techniques for analyzing information and making decisions. However, the foundation for all these skills rests in our ability to create these essential moments of pause and reflection.

We've learned that pausing isn't passive - it's an active tool for better thinking. Regular reflection improves decision-making, and taking time to observe leads to deeper understanding. The best responses often come after a moment of pause. In the next chapter, we'll *throw a ray of Sunshine on our experience as we find optimism and insight, but* remember, sometimes the clearest vision comes when you're sitting still, pausing and reflecting from your mental park bench.

Key Takeaways from Chapter 11

1. **The Power of the Pause** – Taking deliberate moments to pause and reflect helps sharpen awareness, improve decision-making, and prevent impulsive reactions.

2. **The 'Park Bench' Metaphor** – A park bench isn't just a physical place; it's a mental space where one can slow down, observe, and think before acting.

3. **The Three S's of the Park Bench Principle** – *Stop* to pause your thinking, *Sit* to be present with your thoughts, and *Survey* to gain a clearer perspective before making decisions.

4. **Purposeful Pausing in Daily Life** – Pausing before reacting to social media posts, school challenges, or conflicts can lead to better outcomes and deeper understanding.

5. **Reflection as a Tool for Growth** – Regular moments of reflection enhance learning, strengthen critical thinking, and allow for personal development by

reviewing past actions and decisions.

6. **Lessons from Nature** – Just as patient observation reveals deeper details in a garden, taking time to reflect helps uncover patterns in our thinking and emotions.

7. **Pausing Isn't Passive, It's Powerful** – In a world that rushes forward, taking time to stop and reflect leads to clearer thinking, better problem-solving, and wiser decision-making.

REFLECTION EXERCISE

Consider a recent situation where you reacted quickly and perhaps wish you hadn't. Write about:

1. What happened?

2. How did you react?

3. What might have been different if you'd taken a "park bench moment"?

4. How could you incorporate a pause next time?

Chapter Twelve

A Ray of Sunshine: Finding Optimism and Insight

Have you ever noticed how some people find opportunities in every challenge? Or how certain friends always manage to come up with creative solutions when everyone else is stuck? They're not just "lucky" or "naturally positive" – they've developed a way of thinking that helps them see possibilities where others see problems.

Finding Optimism and Insight

The weather felt uncertain as we meandered through the park one cloudy morning. Thick clouds loomed overhead, making the world seem grey and dull. Suddenly, the sun broke through the cover, casting golden light over the lake and the trees. The transformation was breathtaking. The once-muted colors became vibrant, and the warmth lifted our spirits.

This moment reminded me how a single ray of sunshine can shift an entire perspective. Optimism, like sunlight, doesn't eliminate challenges; it provides clarity and hope, encouraging us to see beyond difficulties and find opportunities even in dark times.

Imagine you're trying to solve a puzzle in a dark room. You might have all the pieces, but without light, it's nearly impossible to see how they fit together. Optimism and insight are like turning on a light – they help you see connections and possibilities that were always there, just waiting to be discovered.

Sunset rays peeking over the clouds and through the trees

Fueling Your Insight Engine

Think of your brain as having an "insight engine" – a part that generates new ideas and perspectives. Like any engine, it works better with the proper fuel and maintenance:

1. *Curiosity* - Ask "What if...?" questions, look for unexpected connections, and consider alternatives

2. *Open-Mindedness* - Review different viewpoints, challenge your assumptions, and welcome new ideas

3. *Playfulness* - experiment with possibilities, try unusual combinations, and learn from your mistakes.

The Power of Optimism

Optimism is not about denying reality or pretending everything is perfect. Instead, it's about choosing to focus on possibilities rather than limitations. It's a mindset that sees potential solutions where others might see only problems. Optimism empowers you to move forward, even when faced with setbacks because you believe there's something worth striving for on the other side. It's the key that puts you in the driver's seat of your life, steering you towards your goals.

When you approach life with optimism, you're more resilient because challenges feel less overwhelming when you believe there's a way through. You're also more innovative because a positive outlook inspires creative thinking and solutions. And finally, you're more open to embracing new experiences and ideas.

Like the sunlight breaking through the clouds, optimism illuminates paths that might otherwise remain hidden. Optimism doesn't always mean being happy, ignoring problems, or pretending everything is perfect. It is not about avoiding or ignoring negative feelings when they surface.

Optimism isn't just a perspective; it's a way of living, learning, and growing. Real optimism is about believing in possibilities, seeing setbacks as temporary, looking for opportunities in challenges and maintaining hope while facing reality. At its core, optimism is a choice—a decision to see opportunities where others see roadblocks, to find strength in adversity, and to believe that every day holds the potential for growth and change.

Finding Insight Amidst Challenges

Every challenge carries within it the seed of insight, but finding it requires a deliberate shift in perspective. Here are some ways to cultivate optimism and gain insight from difficulties:

1. *Ask Empowering Questions*: Instead of asking, "Why is this happening to me?" ask, "What am I to learn from this?" or "How might this challenge help me improve?" If you have a growth mindset, you may ask, "What skills am I developing?" and "What doors might this open?" Shifting the focus from blame to growth opens the door to discovery.

2. *Look for the Silver Lining*: Every situation has a positive aspect, no matter how difficult. It might be an opportunity to grow, strengthen relationships, or simply a lesson learned.

3. *Practice Gratitude*: Focusing on what you're thankful for helps shift attention away from negativity. Gratitude is like a beacon of light in the darkness, creating a foundation for optimism by reminding you of the good things in your life. It's a powerful tool that can lift your spirits and fill your heart with hope.

Perspective is everything. Imagine standing at the base of a tree, staring up at its branches. From that angle, the tree might look imposing, its canopy out of reach. But if you climb higher, you appreciate the details. You see the patterns of the leaves, the interconnected branches, and the sunlight filtering through. Likewise, when we face challenges, a closer perspective can reveal insights that weren't visible before.

Practical Tools for Optimistic Problem-Solving

1. The Reframe Game – When facing a challenge, try these perspective shifts:

- Change: "This is really terrible!" to: What can I learn from this?"

- Change: "I can't do this." to: How might I do this differently?

- Change: "Everything is going wrong." to: What's working well?

When stuck, scan your situation for hidden opportunities, such as a chance to learn something new, unused resources like your own skills and knowledge, potential friends and allies who can support you, and alternative approaches that might lead to a solution. Searching for these possibilities is a key aspect of optimistic problem-solving.

2. Building Your Optimism Muscles – Like physical muscles, optimism, and insight get stronger with exercise. Here are some daily workouts:

- *The Good Things Journal* - Each day, write down three things that went well, one thing you learned, and one possibility you discovered.

- *The Solution Safari* - When facing a problem, list all possible solutions (even silly ones) and test and adjust your solutions. Look for patterns in what works and combine different approaches.

- *The Gratitude Lens* - Practice finding the positive by noticing small victories, appreciating progress, and celebrating effort. Remember also to identify and thank your helpers.

The Science of Optimism

Optimism isn't just a feel-good idea; it has real, measurable benefits:

1. *Health*: Optimistic individuals tend to have stronger immune systems and lower stress levels.

2. *Success*: A positive outlook often correlates with higher school, work, and personal achievement.

3. *Relationships*: Optimism fosters better communication, deeper connections, and more fulfilling relationships.

Practicing optimism trains your brain to focus on possibilities rather than problems. This mental shift doesn't mean ignoring difficulties but reframing them as challenges to overcome rather than insurmountable obstacles. Optimism empowers you to approach challenges with curiosity and confidence, seeing them as opportunities for growth rather than barriers to success.

Practical Ways to Cultivate Optimism

1. *Visualize Success*: Spend a few moments each day imagining yourself overcoming a challenge or achieving a goal. This practice trains your mind to focus on positive outcomes.

2. *Reframe Negative Thoughts*: When faced with a setback, challenge yourself to find a more constructive way to view the situation. For instance, if you fail a test, instead of thinking, "I'm terrible at this," try, "This shows me where I need to improve."

3. *Surround Yourself with Positivity*: Spend time with people who uplift and inspire you. Positivity is contagious, and being around optimistic individuals can influence your mindset.

4. *Celebrate Small Wins*: Recognize and appreciate small victories. Every step forward, no matter how small, is progress.

Bringing Light to Others

One key aspect of optimism is its ability to inspire those around you. Like the sun lighting the park, your positivity can brighten someone else's day.

On one of our visits to the park, Shasha noticed a young boy struggling to fly a kite. The wind was unsteady, and his kite kept falling. She walked over and smiled at him, and he was encouraged. Soon, he was flying the kite successfully and even offered her the chance to hold the cord. The boy's face lit up, and so did Shasha's. Her kindness reminded me that optimism isn't just about your outlook—it's about sharing your light with others. Sometimes, your belief in someone else's potential can make all the difference in their experience.

A Ray of Sunshine in Your Life

The moment the sun broke through the clouds in the park was fleeting, but its impact lingered. It transformed how we experienced the day, reminding us of the power of light and warmth.

In your own life, moments of optimism can have a similar effect. They might not eliminate your challenges but can transform how you experience them. Like sunlight breaking through the clouds, optimism reveals beauty, opportunity, and potential that might go unnoticed. Remember to seek out those rays of sunshine as you continue to think critically. They are there, even on the cloudiest days, waiting to guide you toward insight and hope.

Turning Optimism into Action

Optimism is a mindset that becomes most powerful when paired with action. A ray of sunshine doesn't just brighten the sky; it encourages growth, nurtures life, and sparks movement. Likewise, optimism should drive you to take constructive steps, no matter the circumstances. Here's how you can turn optimism into meaningful action:

1. Start with Small Steps: Don't wait for everything to be perfect before taking action. Optimism gives you the courage to move forward, even when conditions aren't ideal. For instance, if you're working toward a personal goal, focus on what you *can* do today instead of what feels out of reach.

2. Model Optimism for Others: When Shasha encouraged the boy with the kite, she wasn't just helping him, she was showing him how to stay hopeful and persistent. Similarly, your actions can inspire optimism in others.

3. Use Optimism to Fuel Resilience: Life will inevitably throw challenges. Instead of being discouraged, let your optimism remind you that setbacks are temporary and solvable.

4. Pair Optimism with Realism: Optimism doesn't mean ignoring risks or challenges—it means acknowledging them while believing in your ability to overcome them. This balance of hope and practicality ensures your actions are inspired and practical.

Reflecting on Your Ray of Sunshine

As we left the park that day, the memory of the sunlight breaking through the clouds stayed with me. It wasn't just the beauty of the moment that resonated; it was the message it carried. Optimism, like sunlight, is powerful not because it removes obstacles but because it reveals paths forward.

Think about the moments in your life when a slight shift in perspective brought clarity or hope. Maybe it was a kind word from a friend during a tough time or a personal realization that turned a problem into an opportunity. Those moments are your rays of sunshine—reminders that there is light to guide you even in challenging times.

The Ripple Effect of Optimism

Optimism doesn't exist in isolation; it spreads. Just as sunlight illuminates everything it touches, your positivity can have a far-reaching impact. When you approach life with optimism, you inspire others to do the same. You create a ripple effect that strengthens relationships, fuels collaboration, and fosters a more supportive environment.

In acquiring critical thinking skills, optimism is a constant ally. It will help you manage challenges, find opportunities, and remain open to new ideas. By cultivating a positive mindset and taking intentional steps forward, you can make optimism a guiding force in every aspect of your life.

Celebrating Your Progress

When we reached the top of the hill, we took a moment to admire the panoramic view of the city. We had made it! The view was beautiful, but the process of getting there mattered most. We learned to evaluate the terrain, make decisions, adjust our approach, and stay focused on our goal.

Just as we celebrated our success at the top of the hill, it's important to celebrate your milestones as you progress toward your goals. Each step forward, no matter how small, is a victory. Recognizing and celebrating your achievements injects sunshine into your life, helps keep you motivated, and reminds you that you can achieve anything you want.

A Final Reflection

As you walk your path through parks, classrooms, relationships, and life itself, remember that the sun is always there, even when hidden behind clouds. Optimism is your reminder to look for the light, even when it's hard to see. Just as Shasha and I found joy in the sunlight breaking through the clouds, you, too, can find rays of hope and insight in your journey. Let those moments fuel your determination, guide your decisions, and inspire you to share your light. Optimism isn't about ignoring the clouds but remembering that the sun is still behind them. With practice, you can learn to spot those rays of sunshine and use them to light your way forward.

Every problem contains possibilities. Every setback holds lessons. Every challenge brings growth opportunities. Your job is to find them – and now you have the tools to do just that. Embrace it, and let it illuminate the possibilities that lie ahead.

Key Takeaways from Chapter 12

1. **Optimism Transforms Perspective**
   Like a ray of sunshine breaking through the clouds, optimism doesn't remove challenges but provides clarity and hope. It helps you see opportunities where others see obstacles.

2. **Insight Comes from the Right Mindset**
   Your brain has an "insight engine" that works best when fueled by curiosity, open-mindedness, and playfulness. Asking "What if...?" questions and challenging assumptions help unlock creative

solutions.

3. **Optimism is a Choice, Not Denial**
   Being optimistic doesn't mean ignoring problems—it means focusing on possibilities and solutions. It empowers resilience, sparks innovation, and helps navigate setbacks with confidence.

4. **Challenges Contain Seeds of Growth**
   Instead of asking, "*Why is this happening to me?*", shift your perspective to "*What can I learn from this?*" or "*How might this challenge help me grow?*" This mindset fosters problem-solving and self-improvement.

5. **Reframing Challenges Leads to Solutions**
   Simple shifts in thinking, such as changing "*I can't do this*" to "*How might I do this differently?*", can open up new possibilities and prevent feeling stuck.

6. **Optimism is a Skill That Can Be Strengthened**
   Just like physical exercise builds muscles, optimism grows stronger with daily practice—keeping a gratitude journal, celebrating small wins, and actively looking for positive aspects in any situation.

7. **Optimism Creates a Ripple Effect**
   Your positivity can inspire and uplift others, just as Shasha's encouragement helped a boy fly his kite. By sharing optimism, you contribute to a more supportive and motivated environment.

Discussion Questions

1. *What's a challenge you faced that led to unexpected*

good results?

2. How do you usually react to setbacks? How might you react differently?

3. Who are the most optimistic people you know? What can you learn from them?

4. How could you help others find opportunities in their challenges?

PART V

REAL-LIFE APPLICATION

Motivation gets you going, passion keeps you growing, but it's persistence that gets you there.

—Andrea Campbell

Chapter Thirteen

The Community Garden: The Power of Collaborative Thinking

As we ventured into the broader park space, we observed groups engaged in various activities across different areas. Some people had spread colorful blankets for a picnic under the shade of oak trees, while others were engaged in an energetic game of frisbee in the open field. Yet others were jogging along the winding paths, and some were strolling, pausing occasionally to observe the wildlife or admire the flowers.

Despite these different purposes and activities, everyone seemed to find their place in the shared landscape, each group adapting to the others in a natural, unspoken choreography, creating a beautiful mosaic of human interaction.

"The bird, Mommy." Shasha had observed that a bird had a broken wing, her eyes taking in the scene with the remarkable attention to detail I've come to appreciate as one of her unique gifts. Where I saw general activity, she noticed movement patterns, details, and people's actions.

Different Minds, Shared Spaces

Watching Shasha comprehend the world has taught me more about thinking than any book or class ever could. Her neurodiverse mind processes information differently than mine, noticing details I miss and making connections I might never consider. In the early years, I mistakenly tried to teach her to think "normally" until I realized that our different thinking styles, when combined, created a more complete understanding than either of us could achieve alone.

The park today offered a perfect illustration of this principle. We approached the community garden and saw a group of teenagers working on a puzzle at one of the picnic tables. One teenager sorted pieces by color, another arranged them by shape, and a third focused on assembling them. Each approach had merit, but their combination led to rapid progress. Their thinking styles didn't compete – they complemented each other.

I saw simply a puzzle being solved; Shasha, saw a ladybird on the shirt of one of the teenagers. Her observation was simple yet profound. Just as her mind and mine function differently but complement each other, these young people brought different strengths to their shared project. None could have completed the puzzle alone in the time they did, but together, they transformed a bag of blocks into something beautiful.

The Limits of Solo Thinking

This experience reminded me of something I've repeatedly observed as a parent and a writer. We all view the world through lenses shaped by our experiences, knowledge, and the unique wiring of our brains. This personal viewpoint helps us make sense of the world but also creates limitations and blind spots in our thinking. In critical thinking, we must stay open to new ideas, be flexible in our approaches, and be willing to embrace change. Just as a rolling stone doesn't stay in one place long enough to gather moss, an open mind doesn't stagnate; it grows, evolves, and thrives.

Shasha works in a team on an outdoor project

The Benefits of Thinking Together

Collaborative thinking offers benefits that individual thought processes, no matter how brilliant, cannot match. First, it brings diverse perspectives to bear on a problem. When Shasha and I experience our day together, her detailed focus and my big-picture thinking create better plans than either of us could devise independently.

Second, collaborative thinking helps identify and correct errors in our reasoning. We all have blind spots—assumptions we make without realizing it or biases that color our judgment. When we think with others, they can gently point out these errors before they lead us astray.

Third, when different thinking styles interact, new ideas emerge that neither person would have generated alone. Shasha's literal interpretation of language sometimes leads to unexpected insights that spark my creativity in new directions.

Digital Collaboration: Opportunities & Challenges

As we paused to rest on a park bench, I glanced at my phone and saw a message from a friend asking me to review her project plan and offer feedback. It struck me how seamlessly collaboration extends beyond physical spaces like this park. In our digital age, technology has transformed the way we think and work together, connecting diverse minds across the globe in ways that were once unimaginable.

Digital collaboration unlocks incredible opportunities, breaking down geographical barriers and allowing us to exchange ideas, learn from different perspectives, and create innovative solutions together. However, it also comes with its own set of challenges. While online spaces can strip away certain biases—focusing more on ideas than appearances—they can also reinforce others. Instead of broadening our perspectives, we may find ourselves in echo chambers, surrounded only by opinions that mirror our own.

Effective digital collaboration requires more than just participation; it demands intentionality. We must actively encourage and appreciate diverse viewpoints, challenge our assumptions, and engage in meaningful discussions that push our thinking forward.

Like a well-tended park that thrives with a variety of plants and wildlife, the most enriching digital spaces are those that cultivate a diversity of thought, fostering true intellectual growth.

Learning to Share Thinking Space

Learning to share your thinking space effectively takes practice. For Shasha and me, it began with genuine curiosity about each other's perspectives. When she sees something differently, I've learned to ask questions rather than immediately correcting her. For example: "What led you to that conclusion? What else did you notice?

Active listening forms another key part of collaborative thinking. As we watched a father and daughter feeding ducks by the pond, I noticed how attentively he listened to her excited observations, giving them the same weight he would give an adult's. Feeding the animals is prohibited at the park, but we do not judge them. True collaboration requires respectful attention, which doesn't always come naturally but can be developed with practice.

The Role of Support Systems

While staying calm, adaptable, and resilient is important, it's equally crucial to have support during times of stress. Storms are easier to weather when you have a network of friends, family, or mentors who can offer guidance, comfort, and encouragement. When we encounter a particularly challenging moment in the park—an unexpected change in weather or a tricky pathway—we always rely on each other. The support we give one another helps us remain calm, focused, and resilient.

Having a strong support system is like having a sturdy umbrella when the rain starts to fall. It doesn't prevent the storm from happening, but it can make all the difference in how you handle it. So, as you face your personal storms, remember that it's okay to lean on others. We all need help occasionally, and reaching out for support is a sign of strength, not weakness.

The Strength of Intellectual Humility

Perhaps most importantly, effective collaboration requires intellectual humility, recognizing that none of us has all the answers. Even experts have blind spots, and those with different perspectives often see what others miss. When Shasha was younger, I sometimes dismissed her literal interpretations of idioms as misunderstandings. I've since learned that her alternative readings often contain wisdom I would never access through my more conventional thinking. Embracing intellectual humility opens us up to a world of new ideas and perspectives.

As the afternoon light began to soften and we started our walk home, I reflected on how our different minds had enriched our shared experience of the park. I had noticed the broader patterns of human interaction; Shasha had observed specific details of plant life and wildlife behavior. We had a more complete understanding than we could have developed alone.

Thinking Together in a Complex World

As you develop your critical thinking skills, remember that some of your most potent insights will emerge not in isolation but in conversation with others, especially those who see the world differently than you do. Surround yourself with diverse perspectives. Ask questions that spark meaningful discussions. Listen to understand, rather than simply waiting for your turn to speak. Express your thoughts with clarity, but remain open to new ideas and the possibility of refining your views.

The strongest thinkers aren't lone geniuses locked away in deep thought—they are connectors. These bridge-builders bring together different perspectives to form a richer, more complete picture of the world. They create spaces where diverse minds contribute their unique strengths, challenging one another to think more deeply and see further.

By learning to share your thinking space, whether in the classroom, with friends, within your family, or in online communities, you develop skills not just for academic success but for making a real, lasting impact in our complex and interconnected world.

Lessons from the Stone and the Tree

In our visits to the park, I've come to appreciate two contrasting symbols: the rolling stone and the rooted tree. We encountered the rocks as we climbed the hill to look around and hugged many trees in the park. The Rolling Stone symbolizes movement, change, and exploration. It teaches us to stay curious, open, and willing to adapt to new circumstances. On the other hand, the tree, with its deep roots and steady presence, represents stability, resilience, and the strength to withstand challenges.

Critical thinking requires both qualities. You need the adaptability of the rolling stone to stay open to new ideas, as well as the stability of the tree to hold your ground when it matters most. When you work with people to bring your ideas to light, you'll encounter both and be well-positioned to handle that scenario.

In the next chapter, "Beyond the Beaten Path," we'll explore how to apply critical thinking to real life. However, remember that adaptation happens faster and more effectively when we don't face changes alone. The thinking space you share with others, especially those who think differently than you do, becomes your greatest resource when managing life's inevitable uncertainties.

Key Takeaways from Chapter 13

1. **Different Minds, Shared Spaces** – People process information in unique ways, and embracing neurodiverse perspectives enriches our understanding of the world. Just as Shasha notices details others might overlook, diverse thinking styles contribute to a more complete picture.

2. **The Limits of Solo Thinking** – Our individual viewpoints help us navigate life, but they also create blind spots. Staying open to new perspectives and being flexible in our approach prevent stagnation and promotes growth.

3. **The Benefits of Thinking Together** – Collaboration combines different strengths, helping to correct blind spots, generate new ideas, and lead to more effective problem-solving than working alone.

4. **Digital Collaboration: Opportunities and Challenges** – While technology connects diverse thinkers globally, it also risks creating echo chambers. Effective collaboration in digital spaces requires deliberately seeking different viewpoints.

5. **Learning to Share Thinking Space** – Active listening and curiosity foster meaningful collaboration. Asking questions like "*What do you notice that I might have missed?*" helps build a culture of shared understanding.

6. **The Role of Support Systems** – Just as storms are easier to handle with an umbrella, life's challenges become more manageable with a strong support network of family, friends, or mentors.

7. **The Strength of Intellectual Humility** – Recognizing that no one has all the answers allows for deeper learning. Being open to different interpretations, even those that seem unconventional, can reveal valuable insights.

Exercises

1. Perspective-Sharing Exercise

- *Pair up with a friend or family member and observe the same scene (a park, a café, or a busy street).*
- *Each of you writes down 5 things you notice.*
- *Compare your lists—what did the other person see that you missed?*
- *Reflect: How do different perspectives contribute to a fuller understanding?*

2. Collaborative Problem-Solving Challenge

- *Gather a small group and choose a problem (e.g., "How can we reduce waste at school/work?").*
- *Assign each person a different thinking role: Big-Picture Thinker, Detail-Oriented Thinker, Skeptic, Optimist, Creative Thinker.*
- *Discuss the problem and see how each role contributes to the solution.*
- *Reflect: How did the variety of perspectives help?*

3. Support System Reflection

- List the top three people you turn to for advice and support.

- Write about a time they helped you see something from a new perspective.

- Identify one way you can be a better support to others in return.

Chapter Fourteen

Beyond the Beaten Path: Applying Critical Thinking to Real Life

As we continued our walks through the park, we often veered off the main trail. The path was familiar, safe, and well-trodden, but we were always eager to explore, to venture beyond the beaten path and discover something new. It wasn't always easy—there were unexpected obstacles, hidden turns, and moments when we weren't sure where we were headed. But those detours often led to new insights, experiences, and perspectives, filling us with a sense of adventure.

Applying critical thinking often requires us to step outside our comfort zones and question the conventional way of doing things. When we follow the beaten path, we stick to what is known, what is easy, and what others have already figured out. But when we step off that path, we invite new opportunities for growth, innovation, and self-discovery.

Thinking Beyond the Obvious

One of the most powerful aspects of critical thinking is the ability to see beyond the obvious. It's easy to follow the well-worn paths, make decisions based on assumptions, or act based on what everyone else is doing. But critical thinking invites us to pause and consider the bigger picture. It asks us to challenge our initial assumptions and explore alternative solutions.

For instance, during one of our walks, we could have taken the most direct route since we understood the park's layout. But by applying critical thinking, we opened ourselves to discovering hidden areas where the view was unexpectedly beautiful or where new birds were gathered in quiet corners. In those moments, we didn't just observe what was before us; we asked questions, observed with intention, and reflected on what we found. This curiosity and questioning mindset allowed us to experience more than surface-level reality.

Similarly, critical thinking helps us see beyond the immediate real-life situation. It's the ability to look at problems from different angles, ask more profound questions, and avoid rushing to conclusions. It helps us resist the temptation to follow the crowd or rely on easy answers. Instead, we embrace complexity and uncertainty, knowing that real progress often lies beyond the familiar paths.

Seeking Solutions in Unlikely Places

We often find ourselves in unfamiliar territory when we venture beyond the beaten path. It's easy to feel lost or uncertain when we stray from the known, but this is where critical thinking becomes most valuable. In these moments, we are challenged to solve problems creatively and adapt to new situations. We learn to navigate uncertainty, find alternative routes, and build resilience.

Take, for example, a problem you might encounter in everyday life—whether it's deciding on a career path, choosing how to spend your time, or resolving a personal conflict. The obvious solutions might be tempting but not the best for you in the long run. Instead of following the path taken by everyone else, critical thinking encourages you to evaluate your options carefully, consider the pros and cons, and think about what truly aligns with your values and goals.

In the park, there was a point when we found ourselves facing a small stream that separated us from a beautiful grove of trees. The easiest path would have been to turn around and head back to the main trail. But instead, we paused and thought about how we could cross. After careful observation, we noticed a few large stones sticking out of the water, forming a natural bridge. It wasn't the obvious solution, and it required a little creativity and courage, but we could find a way forward by thinking critically.

Similarly, when faced with challenges in life, critical thinking can help us find solutions in unexpected places. It encourages us to think outside conventional solutions and look for alternatives others may overlook. It pushes us to trust our ability to think creatively, even when the path ahead seems unclear.

Applying Critical Thinking to Relationships

One of the most important areas in which we can apply critical thinking is our relationships with others. Whether with friends, family, or colleagues, thinking critically helps us communicate more effectively, solve conflicts, and make decisions that strengthen our relationships.

When we encountered the conflict between the birds in the park, we saw firsthand the importance of perspective and understanding. The larger bird might have been acting out of instinct, but the smaller bird's parent was able to approach the situation with a different mindset. Rather than engaging in the conflict, the parent bird intervened in a way that protected its young and avoided escalating the situation.

Critical thinking allows us to assess conflicts with more empathy and understanding in our relationships. It encourages us to step back and ask ourselves: What are the underlying causes of this conflict? What is the other person's perspective? How can I respond to resolve the issue rather than make it worse? This emphasis on empathy fosters a sense of compassion and understanding in our relationships. By thinking critically, we can find solutions to problems that respect our needs and the needs of others. This attitude helps us avoid misunderstandings, reduce stress, and build stronger, more supportive relationships.

Asking Questions to Strengthen Relationships

Questions aren't just tools for understanding the world but also powerful for building relationships. When you take the time to ask someone thoughtful questions, you show that you value their perspective. For example, instead of asking a friend, "What's up?" try something more specific, like, "What's been the highlight of your day so far?" This shows genuine interest and opens the door to a more meaningful conversation.

Living with Intention

Life is not about following the path everyone else is on. It's about creating your trail and making decisions aligning with your values and goals. Critical thinking is a powerful tool that helps you do just that. It lets you step off the beaten path, explore new opportunities, and intentionally navigate life.

Living with intention, guided by critical thinking, means making decisions that are not just easy or convenient, but that align with your long-term goals and values. It's about being mindful of the paths you choose and the decisions you make, and understanding their potential impact on your life and the lives of those around you.

So, the next time you're faced with a challenge or an important decision, remember to apply the principles of critical thinking. Look beyond the obvious, seek solutions in unlikely places, and take the time to reflect on your experiences. The beaten path may seem easier, but the real rewards come from the moments when we think for ourselves and make decisions that reflect who we truly are.

By thinking critically, you empower yourself to live intentionally, solve problems creatively, and take charge of your life. And in doing so, you'll find that the process—though sometimes challenging—is always worth exploring.

Thinking critically doesn't just involve analyzing isolated events or decisions; it's a mindset that influences how we approach every aspect of life. From our daily routines to the larger, more complex challenges we face, critical thinking helps us make informed choices that lead to more fulfilling outcomes.

Applying Critical Thinking to Life Challenges

We often encounter new and unexpected challenges as we explore life beyond the beaten path. These are the moments where critical thinking truly shines. It teaches us to approach unfamiliar situations confidently, creatively, and resiliently. By applying the same questioning, analysis, and reflection we've learned, we can adapt our thinking to whatever comes our way.

For instance, we encountered a large fallen tree blocking our path during our walk at the park. It would have been easy to turn around and follow a different route. But instead, we stood there for a moment and considered our options. Should we go around the tree? Could we climb over it? Was there an opening we missed?

Critical thinking isn't about having the perfect answer immediately. It's about assessing the situation, weighing different possibilities, and choosing the best action. This process is invaluable when faced with career challenges, personal struggles, or societal issues. Critical thinking equips us with the tools to explore all possible solutions, evaluate their pros and cons, and make decisions that align with our goals.

Carve your own path, build your own future

The Ongoing Process of Growth

Applying critical thinking to real life is not a one-time effort but an ongoing process. Just like in our walks, where we continually learn and adjust our approach, critical thinking is a habit that grows stronger with practice. We'll inevitably refine our skills and develop deeper insights as we face different circumstances.

As we continued to walk through the park, I realized that every step, no matter how small, was a part of the bigger picture of our experience. In life, it's the same. Every decision, no matter how seemingly insignificant, contributes to the overall direction of our path. With each opportunity to think critically, we're not just solving problems or making decisions—we're building our resilience, expanding our knowledge, and growing into more thoughtful individuals.

Similarly, when we apply critical thinking to our relationships, we create stronger connections with others. By listening carefully, questioning assumptions, and approaching disagreements with empathy, we deepen our understanding of one another and find more meaningful ways to communicate. Critical thinking allows us to step back from our emotions, consider other perspectives, and act thoughtfully instead of impulsively.

Using Critical Thinking to Overcome Self-Doubt

Sometimes, the steps toward success can feel lonely or discouraging, and it's easy to start doubting yourself. Critical thinking can help you recognize and challenge negative thought patterns. When you face self-doubt, ask yourself: "What evidence do I have to succeed? What have I already accomplished?" Often, we are our own harshest critics, but by practicing self-reflection and applying logic to our fears, we can replace self-doubt with confidence.

The climb up the hill in the park wasn't always easy, and there were moments when Shasha wondered whether we should turn back. But when we encouraged each other and refocused on the goal, our doubts faded, and our confidence grew. Whenever we made it over a problematic part of the hill, it reminded us that we could push through challenges.

Similarly, when you face obstacles, think of the progress you've already made, the skills you've developed, and your resources. Trust that you have what it takes to overcome the next hurdle. And if you don't know the solution yet, that's okay; critical thinking will help you find a way forward.

Building Momentum

As we reached the summit and took in the panoramic view, we felt the sense of accomplishment that comes from overcoming challenges. But the climb didn't end there. As with every successful expedition, achieving your goal isn't a destination; it's a continuous process. Once you reach one milestone, it's time to set your sights on the next.

This is where momentum plays a key role. Critical thinking isn't just about solving problems; it's about creating a cycle of action, reflection, and progress. You keep up your momentum by breaking down larger goals into smaller, manageable tasks and avoiding burnout. Each small success builds upon the last, generating positive energy and motivation.

When Shasha and I reached the top, we didn't stop for long. We enjoyed the view but then took a moment to reflect on what we'd learned during the climb. We discussed what worked well and what could have been done better. This reflective thinking helped us appreciate the process, reinforced the lessons we'd learned, and gave us the confidence to keep moving forward, even after reaching the peak.

Once you've achieved one goal, set new ones. Critical thinking will help you navigate each new goal with the same mindset: methodical, reflective, and resilient. Use each success as fuel for the next challenge, and never lose sight of the importance of growth, no matter where you are in the process.

Staying Calm and Thinking Clearly

Life, much like the weather, can sometimes bring sudden storms. These storms might take the form of unexpected challenges, stressful situations, or difficult decisions that cloud our minds and make it hard to think clearly. The key to navigating these turbulent moments is staying calm and maintaining clarity amid chaos.

In this chapter, we will explore how to weather the storms that come our way by developing the ability to stay calm and think clearly—skills that will help you make better decisions and approach problems with a sense of control. Stress and uncertainty are inevitable, like a sudden downpour or a gust of wind, but how we respond to them makes all the difference.

Staying Grounded: The Role of Your Values

When storms hit, it's easy to lose sight of what really matters. The noise, stress, and chaos can overwhelm us, making it difficult to think clearly. In these moments, staying grounded in your values can help you regain a sense of direction and purpose.

Shasha and I are often reminded of this when we're out in nature. During a storm, the trees bend and sway but remain rooted in the earth. Their roots keep them grounded, allowing them to endure the wind and rain. In the same way, your values act as your roots, anchoring you when the storm of stress or uncertainty threatens to knock you off course.

When faced with a stressful situation, take a moment to reflect on what matters most to you. Is it kindness? Integrity? Resilience? Let these values guide your actions and decisions, giving you the strength to stay calm and focused. You'll find it easier to weather the storm with a clear mind and a strong sense of purpose when rooted in your core beliefs.

The Role of Self-Talk: Managing Negative Thoughts

Negative self-talk is one of the most insidious forces during stressful situations. When the storm hits, our inner voice often becomes critical, questioning our abilities and heightening our fears. It's important to manage your self-talk and replace negative thoughts with positive, constructive ones to stay calm.

When Shasha was learning how to climb the stony hill, she was initially hesitant, fearing she might fall or get stuck. Her inner voice kept telling her that the climb was too difficult. But I reminded her to challenge and replace those thoughts with more empowering ones: "I can do this. I've made it this far, and I can keep going."

Shasha could push past her doubts and complete the climb by changing her internal dialogue. It's incredible how powerful our words can be, especially those we tell ourselves. When you encounter a storm in your life, take note of the thoughts that arise. Are they helping or hindering you? Challenge negative thoughts and replace them with affirmations that remind you of your strength and capability.

The Importance of Flexibility

In addition to staying calm, we must also be willing to adapt to changing circumstances. The weather, for example, is unpredictable. We might walk in the park, expecting sunshine, only to find that a storm has rolled in unexpectedly. Instead of letting this ruin our day, we adjust: we find shelter, take cover under the trees, or perhaps return home if the storm persists. The key is flexibility; being open to change and adjusting our plans accordingly. In the same way, life often throws us curveballs.

Plans might fall apart, opportunities disappear, or unexpected challenges arise. It's easy to get frustrated or discouraged when things don't go as expected, but how we adjust matters most. Flexibility isn't about giving up on our goals but rather being willing to alter our approach when necessary.

Like when the birds take shelter during a storm, we must also learn when to wait for better conditions. This is an essential aspect of adaptability. Sometimes, waiting, recalibrating, and trying again later is better. Other times, it's about adjusting our approach and finding a new route. The most successful people can weather the storm and emerge with newfound clarity and resolve.

Resilience: Bouncing Back Stronger

Resilience is the ability to bounce back from adversity. It's not just about surviving the storm but about coming through it stronger, wiser, and more capable. Think of the trees in the park—after a storm, they might lose a few branches, or their trunks might bend, but they continue to stand. Over time, they may become stronger because of the winds that once threatened to uproot them.

This is the essence of resilience. Life's challenges can shape us, but they don't have to break us. Each storm you weather builds a stronger foundation for your future. You learn new skills, discover hidden strengths, and develop a deeper understanding of yourself and your world. A key part of resilience is maintaining a growth mindset—the belief that we can learn and improve through effort and perseverance. Just as the land recovers after a storm, so too do we, given time and care. Challenges don't have to be seen as setbacks; they can be seen as opportunities to grow.

Keep Climbing

Your path toward success will always be a series of steps, but each step is essential. As we saw from our climb, your individual, mindful choices determine your success. Whether breaking down your goals, re-evaluating your approach, or simply persevering in the face of difficulty, every decision brings you closer to where you want to be.

The important thing is to trust in your ability to move forward, even when the path is unclear. Like the stones in the park, your steps toward your goals will give you stability and guidance. By applying critical thinking, you'll continue to rise, always focused on your next step and never losing sight of the bigger picture. Keep climbing, learning, and, most importantly, believing in yourself.

The Role of Persistence in Success

The climb to the top of the hill wasn't easy. There were moments when we felt like stopping; the climb seemed too complicated. But each time we paused, we reminded ourselves that the view from the top would be worth it.

The same is true for any goal. Success is a long-term endeavor that requires persistence. Critical thinking helps you keep going when times get tough. It teaches you to assess the situation, learn from setbacks, and adjust your approach. When you encounter failure, critical thinking encourages you to see it as an opportunity to refine your strategy. Persistence is not about stubbornness; it's about being open to learning, adapting, and improving.

Success is not about quickly reaching the top of the hill but the climb itself. Every lesson learned, every challenge overcome, and every step taken brings you closer to realizing your potential. With critical thinking as your guide, you'll be well-equipped to achieve your goals and reach new heights.

Adopting a Mindset of Critical Thinking

Critical thinking is a tool for managing challenges and embracing opportunities. Life is filled with both. As we step off the beaten path and explore uncharted territory, we can discover our potential and carve out our future. Critical thinking helps us stay open-minded, resilient, and flexible as we take on new challenges, learn from mistakes, and grow.

Our walks in the park became a learning tool. Every time we veered off the path, it wasn't just about finding a shortcut or avoiding the conventional route. It was about exploring new perspectives, embracing change, and learning to make the most out of every situation. Learn to embrace the unknown. Don't be afraid to take risks, ask difficult questions, and venture beyond the obvious. When faced with challenges, remember that you have the tools to think critically and work your way to success.

Critical thinking allows us to create the path forward, even when it's unclear. It empowers us to take ownership of our life choices, develop the necessary skills to thrive, and, most importantly, live a life of intention and purpose. By applying critical thinking to our daily lives, we can create our own paths, solve problems confidently, and live in a way that's true to who we are.

The world is replete with possibilities and opportunities for growth. By applying critical thinking principles, you will explore new perspectives and discover new strengths within yourself. Don't follow the beaten path if it doesn't align with your purpose—blaze your own trail and let your critical thinking guide you to places you never thought possible.

Key Takeaways from Chapter 14

1. **Step Outside Your Comfort Zone** – Growth and discovery happen when we move beyond the familiar. Critical thinking encourages us to explore new ideas, challenge assumptions, and embrace uncertainty.

2. **Think Beyond the Obvious** – Instead of taking the most direct route, look for hidden opportunities. The best solutions often come from considering different perspectives and questioning the status quo.

3. **Ask Better Questions** – Thoughtful questions lead to deeper understanding and better decisions. Practicing curiosity helps develop problem-solving skills and opens new possibilities.

4. **Exploration Fuels Growth** – Venturing beyond the familiar opens doors to new experiences, insights, and personal growth. As stepping off the main trail led to unexpected discoveries, embracing new challenges fosters critical thinking and adaptability.

5. **Challenge the Obvious** – Critical thinking requires looking beyond the surface and questioning assumptions. Instead of taking the most direct route, exploring alternative paths can lead to better, more innovative solutions.

6. **Embracing Uncertainty Builds Confidence** – Thinking critically helps overcome self-doubt and fear of the unknown. Each challenge faced with logic, reflection, and creativity strengthens the ability to trust one's judgment and manage life's twists and turns.

7. **Living with Intention Leads to Better Decisions** – Rather than following the crowd, critical thinking empowers individuals to make choices aligned with their values and goals. Being mindful of decisions leads to a more purpose-driven life.

EXERCISES

Exercise 1: The Unexpected Connection Challenge

Objective: Develop creative problem-solving by linking unrelated ideas.
Instructions:

- Write down 10 random words (e.g., umbrella, mountain, piano, river, mirror).

- Pick two words at random and challenge yourself to find a connection between them. Example: How is a piano like a river? (Possible answer: Both can flow—music flows like water, and both can be calming.)

- Discuss how this exercise helps in seeing beyond the obvious and making creative connections.

Exercise 2: The Opposite Approach

Objective: Challenge assumptions by considering opposite perspectives.
Instructions:

- Think of a common belief or rule (e.g., "The shortest route is always the best.").

- Now, argue the opposite: "The longest route can sometimes be the best."

- Come up with at least three reasons why the opposite might be true.

- Discuss how this shift in thinking can help with problem-solving and seeing hidden opportunities.

Exercise 3: The Unusual Route Exploration

Objective: Experience firsthand the benefits of stepping off the beaten path.
Instructions:

- Take a walk (either outside or in a familiar place like school).

- Instead of following your usual route, take a different path or explore a new area.

- Observe what you notice that you wouldn't have seen otherwise.

- Reflect on how stepping outside the usual routine can bring new insights and unexpected discoveries.

PLEASE LEAVE A REVIEW

If you found this book interesting, please consider sharing your thoughts by leaving a review on Amazon. As self-publishing authors, we rely very much on reviews. They help our books rank and reach more readers. Leaving a review takes a minute and will make a world of difference. Please scan the QR code or follow the link below. Thank you.

https://mybook.to/rfCNgTS

A GIFT FOR YOU

If you like this content and want to receive our newsletters and be informed of new releases, please join our mailing list by visiting this link or scanning this QR Code. As a thank you for signing up, you can download a set of original inspirational posters that you can print, frame, and position in your favorite space.

http://eepurl.com/h8SU31

Other Books by the Author

https://mybook.to/UwKH32

https://mybook.to/dPluL

https://mybook.to/Otqyd

Please visit my author page for other books:
amazon.com/author/andrea-campbell

Conclusion

As we reach the final pages of this book, I hope you recognize that critical thinking is more than just a skill; it's a powerful tool that will serve you for life.

Inspired by my walks through the nature reserve with my daughter Shasha, the book was designed to help you make your way in the world with confidence, make informed decisions, and approach challenges with clarity and resilience. It is structured around five key secrets—actions that will help strengthen your ability to think critically:

1. *Lay a Foundation for Critical Thinking* – Understanding what critical thinking is and why it matters.

2. *Observe, Analyze, and Understand* – Learning to see the bigger picture and consider different perspectives.

3. *Make Decisions and Solve Problems* – Developing confidence in your choices and overcoming obstacles wisely.

4. *Grow, Adapt, and Build Resilience* – Strengthening your ability to learn from challenges and remain open to new solutions.

5. *Apply to Real-Life* – Applying critical thinking skills to everyday situations, from peer pressure to online safety.

These crucial skills will guide you, not only through your teen years, but also into adulthood. The ability to question assumptions, think independently, and solve problems creatively will help you build strong relationships, and make decisions that align with your values and goals. By applying these principles, you will manage life skillfully and inspire others to think critically and live intentionally.

Critical thinking guides you through the complexities of life, helping you see the bigger picture, overcome bias, and solve problems effectively. More importantly, it encourages you to be open to new perspectives, appreciate different viewpoints, and stay resilient even when things get tough. It's about recognizing that every obstacle is an opportunity for growth and that every decision helps to shape your future. Critical thinking will enrich every aspect of your world. The tools you gained will continue to be useful whether you're solving a problem at school, making career choices, or simply looking to understand the world better. The principles will expand your thinking and understanding and help you approach life with greater awareness and purpose. And when you encounter those inevitable moments where you feel uncertain or overwhelmed, remember the lessons of resilience, perspective, and adaptability.

Critical thinking skill development is ongoing—continually learning, questioning, and adapting. Much like the nature reserve, life is full of different paths, unexpected encounters, and challenge that require you to think critically. There will be times when things seem unclear, when peer pressure pushes you in one direction, or when the online world presents information that isn't entirely trustworthy. But with the skills you've gained, you are now equipped to approach these challenges with a clear mind and an open heart. The path to success isn't always straight, and it isn't always

CONCLUSION

easy, but by embracing critical thinking, you can create your own path—one where you make decisions with purpose, solve problems creatively, and adapt to whatever comes your way. The world has endless opportunities, and with the right mindset, you can traverse any road, no matter how unfamiliar or daunting it may seem.

Thinking critically isn't about being perfect or having all the answers; it's about knowing how to ask the right questions, assessing situations thoughtfully, and remaining open to growth and learning. It's about being both cautious and curious—questioning what seems too good to be true while also embracing opportunities to expand your understanding. It's about making thoughtful, informed decisions, learning from your experiences, and striving to grow. The skill gets stronger the more you use it, and with each challenge you face, you will find yourself becoming a more effective and confident thinker.

The skill doesn't only serve us in challenging times. It's equally valuable when things are going well, helping us maintain perspective, enhance our creativity, and seize opportunities with clarity. Recognize that the critical thinking process is yours to own—a path you create, adapt, and redefine as you grow and evolve. Walk confidently in your ability to think critically, solve problems, and adapt to any challenge that comes your way. Trust in yourself and your critical thinking power. The world is yours to explore, and with a clear mind and a thoughtful approach, there is no limit to what you can achieve.

Thank you for taking this walk with me. May your critical thinking development continue to inspire, guide, and empower you to live a life of purpose, insight, and growth—one that is filled with curiosity, wisdom, light and the courage to think for yourself.

Andrea Campbell, MBA, MA, is a social entrepreneur, linguist, writer and creative thinking specialist. Since publishing her first book in 2010, Andrea has released several bestselling books and articles about special needs parenting, entrepreneurship,. and personal development.

Over the years, she has focused on supporting vulnerable people through education and inspiration. As the mother of a child with special educational needs, she is particularly keen on working with families of children with cognitive disabilities. She developed the Pocket Learner, an award-winning innovative educational set of resources for parents, caregivers and educators of children with special needs.

Andrea has also published several inspirational coloring books, journals, and activity books to empower and inspire people everywhere. She holds a masters degree in Business (Creativity & Innovation) and a Master of Arts – Hons (Translation & Interpreting) degree.

Andrea resides with her family in London, UK where she continues to impact through her writing, training programs, coaching, philanthropy, and inspirational speaking. You may contact her via email at andrea@acttrainingco.com.

RESOURCES

Foundation for Critical Thinking. (n.d.). Critical thinking resources. The Foundation for Critical Thinking. https://www.criticalthinking.org/

Greater Good Science Center. (n.d.). The science of empathy. Retrieved from https://greatergood.berkeley.edu/topic/empathy/definition

Halpern, D. F. (1998). Teaching critical thinking for transfer across domains. American Psychologist, 53(4), 449-455.

Harvard Business Review. (2015, January 26). How to de-escalate tense situations at work. Retrieved from https://hbr.org/2015/01/how-to-de-escalate-tense-situations-at-work

Harvard Business Review. (2019, June 24). The paradox of decision-making. Retrieved from https://hbr.org/2019/06/the-paradox-of-decision-making

HelpGuide. (n.d.). Stress management: How to reduce, prevent, and cope with stress. Retrieved from https://www.helpguide.org/articles/stress/stress-management.htm

Khan Academy. (n.d.). Logical reasoning & critical thinking. Khan Academy. https://www.khanacademy.org/test-prep/lsat/lsat-lessons

MindTools. (n.d.). Conflict resolution: Resolving conflict in the workplace. Retrieved from https://www.mindtools.com/pages/article/newLDR_81.htm

MindTools. (n.d.). Problem-solving & decision-making techniques. MindTools. https://www.mindtools.com/

Negotiation Experts. (n.d.). The five most common conflict resolution styles. Retrieved from https://www.negotiationexperts.com/five-most-common-conflict-resolution-style

Paul, R., & Elder, L. (2014). Critical thinking: Tools for taking charge of your professional and personal life (2nd ed.). Pearson.

Psychology Today. (n.d.). Decision making & problem solving. Psychology Today. https://www.psychologytoday/us/basics/decision-making

Psychology Today. (2014, May 1). The power of positive communication in conflict resolution. Retrieved from https://www.psychology today.com /us/blog/words -matter/201405/the-power-positive-communication-in-conflict-resolution

Psychology Today. (2016, November 28). What is emotional intelligence? Retrieved from https://www.psychology today.com/us/basics/emotional-intelligence

Psychology Today. (2019, September 18). Building resilience: A practical guide. Retrieved from https://www.psychology today.com/us/articles/201909/building-resilience

Stanford Encyclopedia of Philosophy. (n.d.). Critical thinking. Stanford University. https://plato.stanford.edu/entries/critical-thinking/

Stanovich, K. E., & West, R. F. (2000). Individual differences in reasoning: Implications for the rationality debate? Behavioral and Brain Sciences, 23(5), 645-665.

TED-Ed. (n.d.). Critical thinking & problem solving playlist. TED-Ed. https://ed.ted.com/lessons?category=critical-thinking

Tversky, A., & Kahneman, D. (1974). Judgment under uncertainty: Heuristics and biases. Science, 185(4157), 1124–1131. https://doi.org/10.1126/science.185.4157.1124

www.ingramcontent.com/pod-product-compliance
Lightning Source LLC
Chambersburg PA
CBHW070046230426

43661CB00005B/785